Tales
of
Molokai

Tales
of
Molokai
The Voice of Harriet Ne

Stories narrated by
Harriet Ne
Collected and prepared by
Gloria L. Cronin
Illustrated by Terry Reffell

Published by
The Institute for Polynesian Studies • Lāʻie, Hawaiʻi
Funded by
Polynesian Cultural Center • Brigham Young University–Hawaiʻi

Portions of this book were originally published in slightly
different form in *Legends of Molokai,* © 1981
by Harriet Ne, Topgallant Publishing Company, Ltd.,
Honolulu. Used by permission.

These tales are to be understood as imaginative works
whose details should not be expected to conform to
historical and anthropological facts.

Library of Congress Cataloging-in-Publication Data
Ne, Harriet, 1915–1991.
Tales of Molokai : the voice of Harriet Ne / stories narrated by
Harriet Ne ; collected and prepared by Gloria L. Cronin ;
illustrated by Terry Reffell.
p.   cm.
Includes tales by the author first published in 1981 under the
title: Legends of Molokai.
Includes index.
Summary: A collection of traditional Hawaiian legends and
contemporary folktales and stories from and about the island of
Molokai. Includes information about the history and geography of
Molokai and the storyteller's life and philosophy.
ISBN 0-939154-50-1 (pbk. : alk. paper)
1. Tales—Hawaii—Molokai.   2. Legends—Hawaii—Molokai.
[1. Folklore—Hawaii.]   I. Cronin, Gloria L.
II. Reffell, Terry, ill.   III. Title.
GR110.H38N4   1992
398.2'09969'3—dc20   91-41722
                              CIP
                              AC

This book is printed on acid-free paper and meets the guidelines for
permanence and durability of the Council on Library Resources.

Distributed for The Institute for Polynesian Studies by
University of Hawaii Press, Order Department
2840 Kolowalu Street, Honolulu, Hawaii 96822

*For
the children
of Molokai*

Note

The reason that the name Molokai is left without the glottal stop is because my *tūtū wahine* (grandmother) says that when she was growing up in Pelekunu it was never pronounced Moloka'i (Moh-loh-kah-ee), but rather Molokai (Moh-loh-kī). Then in about the 1930s, the name changed to Moloka'i, in part she believes because musicians began pronouncing the name that way. Mary Kawena Puku'i, three weeks before her death, called my *tūtū* and told her that the correct name is Molokai, which means "the gathering of the ocean waters." On the rugged north coast of the island, the ocean slams hard into the *pali*. On the south and east shores, the ocean water glides gently to shore due to the location of reefs at least a quarter of a mile offshore. Hence the name, Molokai, "Gathering of the Ocean Waters."

Edward Halealoha Ayau

Contents

vii

Contents

Tales of Naming

Tales of Long Ago

Tales of the North Coast

viii

Contents

Preface

I collected these stories and the accompanying biographical information on tape during several visits to Molokai between 1982 and 1988.
Dr. Kenneth Baldridge conducted a final series of oral history interviews in 1988. The original tapes and transcripts are deposited in the
archives of The Institute for Polynesian Studies, Brigham Young University–Hawai'i.

Sixteen of the forty-three tales were originally collected and
published as *Legends of Molokai*, with a foreword by Inez MacPhee
Ashdown (Honolulu: Topgallant Publishing Company, 1981). I re-
taped those tales as Harriet Ne told them as well as an additional
twenty-seven stories.

A modern Chinese Hawaiian of her times—a generation that witnessed sailing ships give way to jet airplanes, *poi* and fish to ham-
burgers and pizza, an isolated territory to full U.S. statehood—she
reflects the richness of her multiple heritages.

In the vocabulary of Euro-American scholars, Mrs. Ne's prose narratives comprise myths, legends, and folktales, though the categories often overlap. Her myths usually are based on some fact set in the remote past, depict a different world, and feature nonhuman characters and a narrative style comparable to scripture. Her legends are frequently narrated as fact, set in the more recent past, depict the world of today, combine the sacred and the secular, use human characters, and function like history. The most prevalent category, her folktales, can be taken as either fact or fiction, weave across all time zones and places, are usually secular, include human and nonhuman characters, and function like literature.

To be more precise, the myths recorded here are those prose narratives that are told as truthful accounts of what happened in the remote past and usually embody sacred dogma. Legends and folktales (not always distinct categories) traditionally include a wide variety of stories about migrations, wars, victories, heroes, and ruling dynasties. They also include local history, stories of marvelous encounters and places, ghosts, fairies, magical animals, and exemplary characters. Many function as etiological or explanatory tales about the origins and namings of landforms, animals, plants, natural phenomena, and the origin of human institutions.

Mrs. Ne's stories fit into many of these European categories, yet are always intimately connected to local religious belief and practice. In common with tale-tellers of Western tradition she tells "memorates," or first-person narratives concerning spiritual matters deriving from concrete personal experiences reinforced by sensory perceptions (Lauri Honko, "Memorates and the Study of Folk Belief," *Journal of the Folklore Institute* 1 [1964]: 5–19). In this collection, as in most individual folktale repertoires, the memorates repeatedly reveal situations in which the supernatural tradition becomes actualized and influences human behavior. As such they become the context and often the source of the teller's values.

The traditional Hawaiian classification system is just as relevant to this collection. *Ka'ao* was originally a category of stories in which the imagination plays an important part, while *mo'olelo* encompassed stories about historical figures and events (Martha Beckwith, *Hawaiian Mythology* [New Haven, 1940], 1). Folktales are part of this *mo'olelo* category, as are memorate, anecdote, local legend, and family story. The earlier distinction between *ka'ao* and *mo'olelo* breaks down in modern times, however, with *mo'olelo* now including tales of gods.

Because these two complex and overlapping systems are both relevant, it would be arbitrary and inappropriate to attempt rigid categorization of the individual stories contained here. More useful is an understanding of how oral narratives function generally within human culture. As Neil Postman reminds us:

> Human beings require stories to give meaning to the facts of their existence. I am not talking here about those specialized stories that we call novels, plays and epic poems. I am talking about the more profound stories that make people, nations, religions, and disciplines unfold in order to make sense out of the world. . . . A story provides a structure for our perceptions; only through stories do facts assume any meaning whatsoever. . . . [We] require a story to give meaning to [our] existence. Without air our cells die. Without a story our selves die. ("Learning by Story," *Atlantic* 265 [December 1989]: 122)

All human artistic endeavors, including story-telling, are attempts to understand individuals and cultures. They connect us to our various mythological and historical pasts, offering us both a grounding in our cultural heritage and a chance to comprehend the meaning of self and experience. Story-telling such as Mrs. Ne's helps us experience the deeper human need—as teller or as audience—to combine words for the purposes of order, beauty, and meaning. Hers are significant oral narrative art forms that combine traditional story-telling aesthetics, as well as demonstrate her own artistic sensibility and ethos. Though a cultural key for both teller and listeners, they are also an entertainment and an artistic experience designed to communicate a particular worldview. Through her narratives Mrs. Ne unites time past and time present, the natural and the supernatural, the personal and the heroic, the actual and the mythic realms of experience. She does so with distinctive creativity, grace, reverence, humor, curiosity, and drama.

Clearly then, Mrs. Ne's function within her local Molokai community was in large part mediated through her skills as culture bearer and tale-teller. A gifted narrator, she taught, and still teaches through this collection, the dominant social roles, values, and beliefs of her community. The repertoire of the average community raconteur contains about ten to fifteen legends; Mrs. Ne, however, has forty-three remarkable tales that offer enlightening explanations of numerous phenomena. In addition, the stories present a classic example of the process of self-fashioning through which she achieves a heightened consciousness of her social self within the norms of her local community. She does this by drawing heavily on her own life experience as an expressive resource through which she mediates between herself and her community. Some stories are fact, others are fiction. Regardless, they invoke such timeless themes as the disjunction of appearance and reality, social conformity versus ostracism, the relationship of spiritual to physical health, ethics and correct behavior, the interpenetration of past and present, the relationship of the natural to the supernatural, romantic and spiritual love, local belief and lifestyle. Mostly, however, these stories are paradigms for narrating meaning into both an individual and a group experience as they structure her own and the listeners' perceptions of Molokai life, now and then.

The story of Mrs. Ne's life, how she developed her repertoire of tales, mastered Hawaiian culture, and came to understand the role and the social function of her tale-telling is described in her own words in the Introduction. Hopefully, this firsthand oral history will provide the most authentic context for a fuller understanding of the tale-teller, her tales, and her culture.

As collector of these stories, I am grateful to Mrs. Ne for her great spirit of *aloha* and genuine skill as a modern tale-teller. Thanks are also due to Dr. Jerry K. Loveland, director of The Institute for Polynesian Studies, Brigham Young University–Hawai'i, and the Institute staff and consultants for their constant encouragement, generous funding, and technical support.

Working with Mrs. Ne has been a great privilege. Coming to love her in the course of that experience was inevitable. She treasured this valuable cultural legacy of legends, memorates, and folktales. It was her dearest wish—and mine—that they might provide future generations of young Hawaiians with a record of their precious past and of the living oral culture of Hawai'i. It is my particular hope that they will provide an insight into the mind and heart of a remarkable and gracious woman—modern-day *kumu hula*, tale-teller, historian, *kupuna*, Christian minister, and friend to young and old, Hawaiian and visitor.

Gloria L. Cronin
The Institute for Polynesian Studies
Brigham Young University–Hawai'i

Introduction

The Storyteller

Harriet Ahiona Ayau Ne was born on the island of Oʻahu on October 21, 1915, to Edward Haleaniani Ayau and Olivia Kaleialohaokalahui Townsend. Within four months, by her own account, she was taken to Molokai by her parents and raised there for much of her childhood.

Between the years 1925–26 she remembers attending the Liliʻuokalani School in Honolulu. Later, on Molokai she attended eighth grade at the Hoʻolehua School and ninth grade at the Kaluaʻaha School. After her father was ordained to the Independent Protestant Ministry, the family moved back to Honolulu where Harriet attended tenth, eleventh, and twelfth grades at McKinley High School.

After high school, Harriet Ayau married, divorced and remarried, witnessed the attack on Pearl Harbor in 1941, taught *hula*, and raised a family, returning periodically to Molokai. In the late 1940s she moved back to Molokai for good and provided a lifetime of distinguished service to the Hawaiian community and to the local Molokai community in particular. In recognition of that service she was awarded in 1982 the "Na Mākua Māhalo 'Ia" (Give Thanks To The Elders) award given to distinguished Hawaiian *kūpuna*. Until her death on February 26, 1991, she resided on her Hawaiian homestead on Molokai with her adopted son, Gerald, and his family. During her last years she was still giving service as a minister of the Independent Protestant Church, frequently conducting services and preaching sermons in Hawaiian. In addition, she shared her knowledge of Hawaiian culture and language with residents on the island, took an active role in community affairs, and frequently accepted invitations to tell her stories to local school children and cultural groups.

The Island of Molokai

The island of Molokai, which serves as the locus of most of this collection of memorates, myths, legends and naming tales, is the fifth largest of the Hawaiian Islands. Located in the North Pacific Ocean nine miles from Maui and twenty-six miles from O'ahu, Molokai is shaped like a shoe, about thirty-seven miles long by ten miles wide with an area of approximately 261 square miles. The island's east end is mountainous and lush with large valleys, tapering to a dry tableland toward the west end. The north coast peninsula of Kalaupapa is isolated from the rest of the island by high cliffs.

According to myth, Molokai was born of the mating of the goddess Hina and the supreme sky god Wākea, father of all the Hawaiian Islands—hence the island's famous poetic name, Molokai Nui a Hina, "Great Molokai, Child of Hina."

The oldest known Hawaiian habitation on Molokai is located in the verdant Hālawa Valley on the east end and dates from about A.D. 650. These Polynesians seem to have traveled to the Hawaiian Islands from the Marquesas, with later populations arriving from Tahiti. Settlers cultivated taro, sweet potato, and other South Pacific island staples and fished the seas. Molokai is noted for its fishponds, with about sixty ponds along the shoals on the south coast. The west end of the island is considered by archaeologists to have been one of the major centers for adze quarrying in the islands, the stone being a valuable trading commodity. Early Molokai was also well known for sports and for its religious culture and sorcery, reflected in another of the island's famous poetic names, Molokai Pule Ō'ō, "Molokai, Powerful Prayer." Traditional religious shrines and temples dot the island and famed religious leaders included the sixteenth-century prophet Lanikāula and the priests of the Kālaipāhoa (poisonwood gods) of Maunaloa.

It is reasonable to assume that the traditional Polynesian practice of story-telling and oral transmission reached a high level with this culture as a means of preserving history, reciting genealogy, and entertaining the nobility, as well as preserving the mythology of sacred origins through which the Hawaiian high chiefs traced their descent from the gods. Poetic epithets were commonly used to link places and people to myth and history.

The late eighteenth century marks the beginning of Hawai'i's—and Molokai's—modern history. In 1778 Captain James Cook discovered the Hawaiian Islands for the Western world, although Molokai itself appears to have been unvisited by Westerners for many years. But by 1795 the Hawai'i Island chief Kamehameha I had united most of the islands for the first time into one kingdom. Within two decades a thriving sandalwood trade developed along the coastal areas of Molokai, bringing with it the eventual establishment of the first Protestant mission in Kalua'aha in 1832. At this time the resident population was numbered at approximately five thousand. Cattle and sheep were introduced to the island. Kamehameha III provided for the private ownership of land in 1848; the Great Māhele (land division) of that year was a major catalyst for speeding social change, not the least of which was the appearance of leprosy (now called Hansen's Disease) in the other islands and the establishment on Molokai of the infamous Kalaupapa leper colony in 1864. It was here that the now legendary Father Damien de Veuster came in 1873 to care for the outcasts.

Before Prince Lot Kamehameha, also called Kapuāiwa, became King Kamehameha V in 1863 he vacationed on Molokai, and during his nine-year reign he spent his summers here. By the late 1870s most of the large tracts of land in the central and west portions of the island had been formed into His Majesty's Ranch on Molokai, which became the present-day Molokai Ranch.

The annexation in 1898 of the Hawaiian Islands to the United States as a territory spurred pineapple and honey industries on Molokai. Later, pineapple raising grew in importance with the development of irrigation and the appearance of Libby, McNeill and Libby and the California Packing Corporation (Del Monte) plantations. Immigrant Japanese and Filipino plantation workers were brought to the island.

In 1921 the Hawaiian Homes Act passed by the U.S. Congress established the Hawaiian Home Lands. Certain lands ceded by the Crown at the time of Hawaii's annexation were set aside for exclusive homesteading by native Hawaiians. Farming was encouraged by distributing lots with ninety-nine-year leases at low rents. Many small farms were created in Kalama'ula and Ho'olehua for lease to persons of at least 50 percent Hawaiian ancestry, including Harriet Ne's father, Edward Ayau. This enabled the dwindling Hawaiian population of Molokai to reestablish an agrarian base, and along with it, renewed involvement in traditional life-style and customs.

Molokai, perhaps more than the other islands, has preserved much of its cultural knowledge. The road from Kaunakakai to Maunaloa was not paved until 1948, and it was not until 1973 that this almost-untouched modern Hawaiian culture experienced its first major tourism development, begun by the Kaluako'i Corporation and marked by the subsequent opening of the Sheraton Molokai Hotel in 1977. Today the island, nicknamed "The Friendly Isle," has a population of about 6,900 people and remains primarily rural. The land is mostly forested or in agriculture or pasture; the Molokai Ranch is the second largest cattle-raiser in the state and now contains a two thousand-acre wildlife park. The largest town on the island is Kaunakakai, three commercial blocks long and architecturally reminiscent of early twentieth-century Hawaiian towns with wooden false-front buildings. Since 1982, when the last of the pineapple plantations on the island closed, the economic life of the island has shifted to include increasing tourism, general agriculture, and cattle raising.

It is within this rich and particularized historical and social context that the following oral history of one of Molokai's most distinguished modern culture bearers should be read. This oral history of Harriet Ne's life was collected in a series of interviews conducted between 1982 and 1988 on Molokai. Most of them took place in Mrs. Ne's yard, others while sightseeing around the island by car, some in Kaunakakai, and others at the Sheraton hotel. The final oral history interviews were conducted at the Kaunakakai Latter-day Saint chapel. This brief oral history provides the necessary preface and context for the body of stories that follows.

My Molokai Memory:
An Oral History of Harriet Ne

Tell us about the first six years of your life in Pelekunu Valley from 1915 until 1921.

My parents lived in Pelekunu Valley on the northeast coast of Molokai until my mother became pregnant with me. My grandfather, Captain [George] Townsend, captain of the ship *Aikāne*, carried my mother on board ship to Honolulu where I was born in 1915. When I was four months old, my mother brought me back to Molokai to live in Kamalō with my grandmother [Lu'ukia Holau Townsend] until I was old enough to be dedicated to the Lord. Soon after that I was taken to Pelekunu. We lived there for the next six years.

To go to Pelekunu by sea, you have to leave before August 18. After that the ocean is too rough to land a boat on the rocky beach. We had a family trail in the back of Kamalō by Ioli Gulch, which led up to the ridge where there were three big boulders supporting a stick with a white flag. We used the flag to signal the family down at the coast. The pack horses would come back to the house once we reached the bottom of the trail. Then we would walk on by foot. The first five miles is on marshy ground.

Molokai has large tree ferns, larger than Hilo, so we had to get out of this marshy area before sundown. If we slept there we risked attack by wild pigs. It was always raining, so we would pull a branch from above and shelter until daybreak when the pigs disappeared. From the top of the hill we could see all the way down to the valley of Pelekunu. After having taro and dried fish for breakfast, we would make the final descent.

Can you describe the everyday life at Pelekunu in those early years?

We always got up before daybreak because Pelekunu Valley is so narrow that when the sun comes up it shines in there for only a couple of hours before going on to the next ridge. The women, children, and girls used to take the laundry down to the stream, wash the clothes, rinse them, and peg them out on the grassy area with rocks.

The men folks used to get up early too. For breakfast we all drank this *ti nehe*, a Hawaiian tea that is also called Spanish needle. We also had pieces of taro and dried fish.

Then the men would go to work in the taro patches and the women would do chores around the house.

They often sent us children to get *lau hala*. We had to walk around the coastline to Hāka'a'ano even though the *lau hala* there is very brittle from the sea spray. We would gather as much as we could, roll it up, tie it on our backs, and then walk back to the house, where my

mother would teach us how to strip, soften, and tie it into bundles. It was the chore I didn't like because I always got cut with the thorns, so when it was time for *lau hala* picking I used to run off down to the taro patches with my Chinese godfather, Lau Mun [Ah Mun Lau], and hide.

By about 9 A.M. some of the women would prepare lunch. They would usually boil *hīhīwai*, mix *poi*, and broil fish caught in the stream. They also prepared guava, mountain-apple, or whatever was in season.

Usually after lunch the children would play, go fishing or swim. The men would often go upland to lay traps to catch wild pigs. Others would rest or catch up with chores.

Around 5 P.M., everybody would go down to the sea to bathe. The children would go first, then the young people, and finally the adults.

Dinner was usually around 6 P.M. We ate sweet potato, *poi*, raw fish with *limu*, or cooked shellfish. We also ate *ung choi* or swamp cabbage which grew wild in the taro patches.

After dinner, the family and neighbors would gather around and listen to the Hawaiian Bible being read. The religion in the valley was Kalawina, Calvinism. After the coming of the missionaries, people would travel for miles to the church at Kalua'aha on the eastern part of Molokai.

What were the farming methods used at Pelekunu?

Lau Mun introduced many progressive ways of living in Pelekunu Valley. He had my Grandfather Townsend bring water buffalo from O'ahu on board the *Aikāne*. Then he built a wooden plough so that he could cultivate more ground. All eight families in Pelekunu were related in one way or another, so we used to share the buffalo and the plough to plow up our *lo'i* and to plant our taro.

Tell me about the fishing.

Fishing was always important. We liked a variety of fish because our meals consisted mostly of fish, taro, and *poi*. There were certain days that the men went fishing. They knew the exact seasons for *'ōpelu*, *moi*, and other favorite fish. When they caught fish, they would bring it in and give every family a portion according to its size. On days they couldn't catch any fish, we always had the eel cave. Down in there, the men would crunch up shellfish, throw it in, and wait for the eel to jump open-mouthed at the shellfish floating on top of the water. When the eels came up, the men would shove bamboo poles down their mouths and flip them onto the shore. We always rubbed salt on the skins because eel has a funny smell. Later, we rinsed them in salt water, cut them in little squares like soda crackers, added more salt, and dried them in the sun for twenty minutes. Finally, we cooked them on charcoal.

What kinds of activities and recreational interests did the families have?

During the first period of my life in Pelekunu Valley, I began to learn *hula*. At Pelekunu, dancing was always a major activity. My uncles were training to be *hula* dancers with their teacher, Ka'ō'ō. He was the famous *kumu hula* who taught the *hula ku'i*, the special Molokai step for the *hula*.

Only men were dancing the *hula* when I began to learn. I was the only female or young one allowed to enter into the *hālau*. They taught me the *hula* because, while my three uncles were learning, I hung around outside and memorized their password, steps, and ancient *aloha* chants. I was just four years old. One day, Ka'ō'ō caught me at the entrance listening and invited me in. I spent about three months observing and memorizing, then Ka'ō'ō had me get up and dance. It was then he began to teach me the very strenuous *ku'i* step. I practiced and practiced, and pretty soon he had me join the class.

My uncles were very ashamed because I learned faster than they did. They begged my grandma to make me stay away. My grandmother laughed and said, "No, it's going to do her some good when she gets older."

Kaʻōʻō was the best *kumu hula* on Molokai, and I studied under him until I left Pelekunu. When I went to Honolulu as a high school girl, I continued with *hula* lessons, even though everybody teased me about my big hands and clumsiness. The total number of years to become an instructor then was seven years, so I continued until I graduated and became a *kumu hula* as my granduncle had prophesied at Pelekunu.

We were trained better in the old days before Maiki Aiu and ʻIolani Luahine died. I actually stayed with ʻIolani for three months while she trained me to do the *ʻōlapa* and the old-fashioned *hula*. But I didn't want to continue because there were too many *kapu*s and I was a Christian. I couldn't keep the *kapu*s of the ancient Hawaiians, and I made that clear to ʻIolani. She said, "Well, stop now. Quit. That's as far as you go. You know the fundamentals and that's enough." So I quit learning from her.

When did you learn to speak Hawaiian, and how did you gain an education?

All these families at Pelekunu were Hawaiian and Hawaiian was our only language. I spoke it fluently up until I was six years old. By then I had one sister and two brothers, so my father decided we all needed an education. But my mother objected. "They don't need a formal education. All they need to learn is how to plant taro, how to pound it into *poi*, and how to catch fish." My father argued that if anything happened to them, we would need an education.

In 1921, my father finally convinced Mother to move from Pelekunu back to Oʻahu, to Honolulu. We lived up at Pauoa where my father bought some land. He had six taro patches back in there so my mother would feel at home.

At first nobody spoke to us, so we had to learn the English language. I would speak some English and then I would revert back to Hawaiian. Later, as a high school student, I had to relearn Hawaiian.

How did you come to learn Chinese?

When I was eight years old, my Chinese godfather took me away from my mother and father and raised me. My mother objected but my father, being [part] Chinese, said it would be good to expose me to the other side of the race. So, I lived with my Chinese godfather and learned to speak Chinese very fluently.

I was his pride and joy. When we ate in the local restaurant, he used to tell me to order the food so he could hear me rattle off the menu in Chinese. The waitresses used to marvel.

When I was ten years old, I went back to my parents and the family moved to Kaimukī. We all went to Liliʻuokalani School for a couple of years. There were four of us then; the fifth child was not born on Molokai until later. Everyone else was born in Kamalō or Honolulu, even though my mother was one of the original settlers of Pelekunu.

What was the family doing after you left Kaimukī?

I came back to Molokai to live. My father read a notice about Hawaiian homestead lands being open to those who qualified. He applied and got the homestead at Kalamaʻula, so we all came back to Molokai as pioneer homesteaders.

My most vivid memories of that period were of helping my Grandma Townsend oil her four-poster *koa* bed with little flannel bags that we would dip into *kukui*-nut oil. It took hours because of the carvings in the headboard. When my Grandmother Townsend died, she had twenty-one granddaughters; but she told my grandfather, "When I pass away, you give this bed to Harriet."

"Oh no," he protested. "We better give it to Lei, she's the oldest granddaughter."

"Oh no," my grandmother insisted. "Harriet is the only one who has helped me to clean and preserve this bed all these years."

We all lived in one house—my Townsend grandparents, my parents, my brothers, my sister, and my mother's four brothers.

Introduction

Tell me about your school days.

I was tardy to school all the time because when the bell rang I was out on the side of the road on my hands and knees following the bugs or ants creeping around in the grass. I used to get my clothes dirty before I even got to school. My mother spanked me when the teachers reported that I was always tardy and dirty.

During recess or lunch we used to pick rose-apples and throw them at one another. We played a lot of marbles, and we had wooden stilts to walk on. We also loved baseball. At home I would help my mother cook. We used to make stewed guava for breakfast, and if we had the money to buy the sugar, we would make some guava jam.

When I was twelve, I chipped my spine falling off a horse. It was only the Hawaiian medicine that healed it. Bessie Makekau took care of me until my spine was healed.

I belonged to the Girl Scouts in Hoʻolehua, and we used to go down to Kalaupapa, the leper colony, to roll bandages at the longhouse where they separated the leper women from their newborns. We used to walk down the cliff trail every week to roll bandages. When I saw my first leper, I was very frightened because their eyebrows seemed to hang over their eyes. After that I went to Kalaupapa many times.

My mother taught me how to cook when I was just a young girl. Finally, I got so good at baking muffins that my father, who was a supervisor for Libby McNeill, got me to make coffee, muffins, and honey for the workers coming home at six o'clock in the evening. We had a stand on the highway. We were doing really well until somebody complained to the Hawaiian Homes [Commission] because the way station was on Hawaiian Home Lands.

How did your family become such committed Christians?

It began with my Grandfather Townsend. He landed in Pelekunu when his boat was shipwrecked with a little Bible in his hip pocket. My grandmother's family took him in and took care of him. Every day he used to read the Bible to my grandmother. Of course, she didn't understand much English; so when he finally married her, my grandfather asked my great-grandmother, "What do you want me to bring you when I take the ship back to San Francisco?" (He was with the Alaska Steamship Company then.) She said, "Oh, bring my daughter some yardage so she can make herself a new *mu'umu'u*. But I want a Hawaiian Bible so I can read it to my people."

In San Francisco he didn't have much trouble getting the yardage from Chinatown for my grandmother, but he couldn't find a Hawaiian Bible for my great-grandmother. Then somebody told him to go to Sacramento where he met a woman interested in Hawai'i. She knew of a Hawaiian Bible in the local library. So he went to the library and found it had been printed in Tennessee. When he finally got the Bible, he had been gone so long, my grandmother thought he had deserted her. But finally he came back with the Bible.

My great-grandmother used to blow the shell every evening and all the people from the village would come down and sit out on the lawn while she read from it. That's how they first learned about the Lord. They would compare scriptures on the creation to the *Kumulipo,* the Hawaiian creation chant, and to our modern-day life.

How did the Depression affect people at Ho'olehua?

Everyone there was on homestead lands, of course, and we just kept farming. My father, in addition to working for Libby McNeill, was raising corn and watermelon. One season when he had a particularly good crop of corn, Governor Wallace R. Farrington came over and commended my father for it. He also planted sweet potatoes and cucumbers. The Secretary of Interior, Hubert Works, came over once during the Depression years and gave a citation to my sister because she had planted a record crop. They even took pictures of my sister dressed in my father's baseball suit. My mother was upset about this, but we didn't know that the Secretary of Interior was very well known and that we should dress up to honor him.

Even though the Depression years were very bad in Ho'olehua, people loved and shared with one another. One planted corn, one pumpkin, the next one sweet potato. We shared when we harvested. We didn't have taro up at Ho'olehua at that time, so we made *poi* out of pumpkin. We boiled and pounded the pumpkin and mixed potato starch and hot water into it until it thickened. Then we stretched it for *poi.*

My father was the only homesteader who owned a truck. It was an old abandoned Love's Bakery truck that my father had fixed up. He would go from house to house saying, "I'm going to Kaunakakai shopping today. What do you want me to buy you?" If people wanted to go, they got on the truck; if not, they just gave him the money and the shopping list. My father was very friendly with Chang Tung, the owner of the store. He used the Chinese technique of bargaining to lower the price until he could buy the groceries, because some of the people did not give him much money. We all shared with one another. It did not matter if you were a Catholic, a Latter-day Saint, or a Protestant.

I suppose the Depression didn't affect us too much because we never thought we were poor. My father had brought us up to be contented with what we had. The Hawaiians say " *'Olu'olu ka mea loa'a*" (Be contented with what you have). During the Depression years, luckily my father kept his job and we kept our way of living.

By 1928 when I was about thirteen, I finished eighth grade up at Ho'olehua, and went into ninth grade up at Kilohana at Kalua'aha School. I went to the east end and lived with the Wong Hee family and walked from Kamalō to Kalua'aha every day to school. When I finished ninth grade, I went to Honolulu to McKinley for tenth, eleventh, and twelfth grades. One brother stayed on the homestead and another worked so my older sister Lei could go to the University of Hawai'i. My father decided to get a centrally located house so my sister could walk to the university and I could walk to McKinley. So he made a bargain for a house in Pāwa'a, with a Mr. Nekemoto. I got a job after school babysitting for a Navy ensign every day from 4 to 8 P.M.

I graduated from high school in 1932. My sister was eventually a sergeant in the Honolulu Police Department. When she got this steady job, my father didn't have to send payments for the house. He said that after we were through using the house for going to school, it would be used to give each child a start when they got married. Each of the children lived in that house for a year.

Tell me about your young married life after you graduated from high school.

In 1933, I got married and lived in Honolulu. So for part of the Depression years, I was living in Honolulu with my first husband, Paul Kamohoali'i Hapai, Anna Lou's father. Anna Lou was born in 1934 in Honolulu. During these years I was also teaching a class on *hula.*

Did you do other work during those years?

I worked at Pālama Settlement. I was assistant to Annie Kerr, the dental hygienist. Then I took a civil service job working at the Waimano Home for retarded people for three years.

During these years, three more children were born on O'ahu. After I returned to Molokai, I had a miscarriage. Some time later we adopted our nephew, who now has the Kalama'ula homestead.

How long did you live over there on O'ahu?

Only about four years. Then the family asked me to come to Molokai to take over my aunt's homestead. So I asked my husband at that time, Mr. Hooper, who was working at Honolulu Gas Company. He said he wanted to work outdoors, so we moved back to Molokai and we got our own homestead at Ho'olehua. I got a job with the Department of Education in adult education and continued teaching *hula* at night.

When my husband died, Anna Lou had just turned twenty. So I turned the homestead over to her for a dollar and love and that's the homestead she has today. I moved to Kalama'ula because I married Jacob Ne.

Do you remember Father Damien's exhumation in 1936?

I was able to see the ceremonies when they brought his remains in to the Fort Street Catholic church [Cathedral of Our Lady of Peace, in Honolulu]. There was a very large crowd gathered there, and we had a hard time getting through. They had the St. Louis School band playing, and the Sacred Hearts Academy girls singing. Then they brought his remains inside to where all the Catholic fathers were dressed in their regalia.

They had asked to have state dignitaries present. There were Belgian flags on the street. It was no more Damien from Kalawao, it was Damien from Belgium. Before that, they didn't even want to let people know that he was from Belgium. But that day, they hooted and howled that he had come from Belgium, that he was born in Belgium, and that they were taking his remains back to Belgium.

They had a parade in the streets with a black hearse with a rider on the top and men holding flags. Many men were dressed in Catholic clothes and robes from the Order of the Sacred Hearts. I remember that they flew Sister Marianne down. But she didn't want to ride in the parade. She said she would walk. So she walked with the rest of the order. She was wearing a black habit and a black hat. I remember her shoes. She had high boots, and they were so highly polished they shone as she walked with the rest of her order. I guess they had reserved seats in the cathedral because they walked in and they took special seats.

Then they had Mass. It was quite lengthy. I left before they were finished because it was class time and I had to go. I still remember the pomp and circumstance.

Harriet Ne

When you were raising your children, did you continue with hula?

By then I had my own *hālau*. I taught *hula* in my garage because we didn't own a car on Oʻahu. I taught nineteen children and seventeen adults in all on Oʻahu. The adults usually didn't finish the class because they were all mothers with too many interruptions. When I came back to Molokai and took over my aunt's homestead, I began another *hālau*, primarily for children.

Were you in Honolulu when Pearl Harbor was attacked?

I was in Honolulu when World War II broke out in 1941. We had a two-story house and from the second story I could see the bombs blasting away in Pearl Harbor. The women in my neighborhood were terrified because all their husbands were at work. I had the largest house, so all the families came to me for comfort. It was a horrible day. The babies were crying every time another bomb burst. I had a young baby, too, and yet I had faith in the Lord that He would keep us safe.

During the remainder of war, I worked for the U.S. Navy, developing photographs at night. A guard picked me up in the evening and brought me back at one o'clock in the morning. My second husband, Mr. Hooper, worked for the county driving around in blackout trucks with blue lights. I still was not terribly afraid. I always believed that the Lord would take care of us. But the food situation was so bad my father shipped us rice from Molokai by mail.

When the mailman brought the rice bag, all the neighborhood women would rush over to my place with their pots and pans begging for rice. I tried to share as much as I could. There were Japanese, Hawaiian, Portuguese, and Chinese families on that street. We were all short of food and tried to care for each other during those difficult years.

Tell me more about your continuing experience teaching hula *and* Hawaiiana.

When I started teaching *hula* I concentrated on our Hawaiian children. I wanted them to perpetuate the culture. I would select students for a *hula* class by studying them to see if they were soft, or humble, or rugged by nature, or whether they were wicked, or cross, or loved flowers and nature. They had to learn the password. I didn't mind teaching non-Hawaiians because if they were serious they could be adopted into the culture. When my students were ready to graduate I gave them a Hawaiian name to fit their personality.

I trained them for two hours at a time with a break after one hour. They had to work at home on special exercises and on the steps. I also wanted them to practice chanting and get the pronunciation right. In later years, they did it on tape. When they had personal problems that interfered with their learning, we talked about it.

The step invented here on Molokai is especially strenuous. We worked very hard at that. I really tried to know my students because I was their *kumu hula,* counselor, physical exercise specialist, mother, father, and friend.

The theory involved in *hula* is important. You must be relaxed emotionally and clean inside. This means spiritually clean and physically clean. You must eat the right foods. People who eat sweet and fatty foods tire very easily. You must think the right thoughts. You must be able to appreciate nature.

During part of this time I worked for the Kamehameha Schools' Extension Department teaching Hawaiiana in the different elementary schools. Later on, Maui Community College hired me as an Hawaiiana specialist and I taught adult education classes at night. During those years I traveled around to the schools teaching Hawaiian history. Then, if we got through early enough, I would teach a dance or a Hawaiian song. I was very interested in action songs so I used to teach them songs and do the actions for them.

While I was working for Kamehameha Schools I became disabled, so I had to give it up. About then Mr. Pau'ole, the general chairman of the cancer society, asked me if I would be his secretary for the cancer campaign. I also worked with the blood bank. Then I worked with 4-H youngsters and leaders for nearly twenty-three years.

Tell me about the famous trip around the island with Thurston Twigg-Smith, Bob Krauss, and Walter Ritte when you were in your sixties.

That was a great experience. We walked much of the coastline of Molokai. We started walking early in the morning, and I said to Bob, "You aren't going take anything with you?" "No, no, no, we are not taking any food or water. We'll eat what we find on the way." So we started walking at the west end.

When we got down to the southwest point, Ka Lae o ka Lā'au, Bob Krauss said he was hungry and thirsty. We drank from a spring by cupping our hands under the stone and catching the drips. Then he said he was hungry, so we picked wild *'ilima* blossoms growing on the seashore. Later, as we were walking, we came to some *hinahina* plants growing on the side of the beach. I rinsed some in the salt water and had him eat it. It is good for gout and arthritis. He ate quite a big bunch of it.

The rest of the hikers were wondering what we were doing. Finally, one of the Japanese boys came up complaining of hunger. I told him to eat the *'ilima* blossoms. He was hesitant at first, but then he decided he liked it and went off to pick more. So, every place we went, I would find something new for them to eat.

When we came to Wai a Kāne where there's a fishpond with a great many eels, I offered them some eel. But before I could stop them, some went straight into the fishpond to catch crabs and get seaweed. You should have seen the sixteen boys hopping over the wall. They had never seen a place with so many eels. I scolded them and told them that the eels are the protectors of strangers going into Wai a Kāne. When we came to Pālā'au, the dry area, they put crabs in their pockets so they could nibble on the legs. By the time we got to Kalama'ula, they had eaten most of their crabs. When we came to the Coconut Grove, somebody climbed up and got some coconuts to eat.

When we got to Oneali'i Park they were full. That's where the truck with the food was waiting for us. There were about thirty-five people on that trip.

How long did you travel with the group?

Many days. From Kaho'olawe, we came to Molokai, then we walked around the island. Then I went to Lāna'i.

When did you become the recognized historian of Molokai?

It was in 1964. I was commissioned by Governor John Burns to be the historian of the island of Molokai. They felt that I was qualified to be the historian because I have lived in almost every district. I knew the life-style of the island, and I knew most of the *kama'āina* families. It's a job that I really enjoyed because it made me do research and learn more about my island.

When most people think of history, they think of thick books and footnotes. But your history is different!

My Molokai legends are all about the places I have lived around the hundreds of miles of Molokai coast. I have gathered these stories all my life. I have an exceptional memory, and I also have a gift for Hawaiian language. And people listen. They beg for more! How many historians can say that? When I am invited to Scout camp they always beg for spooky stories. I start out with mild ones and then tell spookier stories as the night goes on.

I tell these tales at family gatherings when we talk story. I also tell them at the elementary schools and at small gatherings in the local library. I tell them often to my grandchildren. Many organizations ask if I will come and tell them stories. I also tell stories at the Head Start schools.

When I do this I try to tell them something they can use in their daily lives. I am now called the community pillar. On the east end of Molokai, they call me *kūkū*, *tūtū*, or Auntie Harriet. I preach and I teach Molokai history and Hawaiiana. (I'm still a preacher, you know.) I like to tell stories with a moral to them. I especially like to tell stories about family love and reconciliation in the community or about obedience. I counsel and advise our young people in their way of life. I want them to be proud of being Hawaiian, and to accept the traditions and the *kapu*s of old and apply them in modern life.

I constantly teach my grandchildren values while I'm talking story. I teach them things like the importance of *hānai*. I teach them respect for their elders. The story gets longer when they say, "Why did they have to do that? Why was it the custom? How come it's part of our culture?" So then I have a chance to explain.

I often tell one about a Hawaiian princess who wanted to go out to play but had to stay inside and sew. She was so angry her eyes were blinded by tears and she pricked her finger. The blood dropped into the center of a hibiscus flower, which immediately became red. The moral of the story is to be obedient and never to do anything in anger. Everything must be done as an act of love and service. I like to tell the children the legends of Hina. I also like to act the stories and use my hands skillfully during the telling, by way of talking story.

What exactly is "talking story"?

Mo'olelo is formal story-telling, but talking story is different. It is most often done when families get together for a family reunion or a family dinner. Lots of families meet after church and talk story. In our family, my daughter comes after church and brings her potluck, along with the other daughter and my son. Then we all eat together. They usually ask me to tell them stories of when I was young, of my grandmother and grandfather, and of the life at Pelekunu. It seems to bring them closer. I know my children love to hear these talk stories because they never met Grandma and Grandpa Townsend, who died before they were born. It gets the generations closer together.

In ancient traditional Hawaiian culture, they had a person who was an official storyteller. His responsibility was to tell stories only in the court because he was an official storyteller for the *ali'i*. The court storyteller also had to amuse the chiefs by telling whatever stories were requested. The court liked to hear spooky stories, and sometimes they would request stories about Pele.

They also made up jokes which were passed on by word-of-mouth. The jokes and stories would go from one court to another and even to the different islands. The stories also would go on and on through time and place. Maybe a story would originate on Molokai; by the time it got to Hawai'i, a lot would have been added.

Somebody else other than the storyteller would then be assigned to recite the genealogies. There is a body of legends about the gods that Hawaiians have kept alive. These court storytellers had to remember all the Māui stories, all the Hina legends, and all the creation stories.

The storytellers were recommended by a *kahuna*, then they were put to a test. After the training period, the *ali'i* would choose among them. They would look for a person whose range was flexible—one who wouldn't lean too much towards the Pele stories or any other group of tales. Such a person had to be able to sing and add some parts of the story on his own. He also had to know the songs and be able to chant. Often stories would be chanted first in a singsong voice. Then the tale-teller would talk, and then he would sing again. Tale-tellers also used dramatic gestures. They would be credited for memorizing the exact words that a certain god or character said. It all had to be memorized very carefully. If the storyteller said the wrong word in the wrong place, it changed the entire meaning of the sentence.

There were punishments for those who weren't good at story-telling or who forgot. If it was discovered that there was an error, the storyteller would be banned from the court. He was not allowed to come there anymore. His reputation would go ahead of him, and others would know that he was not a true storyteller. It is just like being hired for entertainment. If you can't give a good performance, then your bad reputation travels ahead of you.

To me, the good storyteller speaks with his eyes and motions with his hands. His eyes must reflect sadness and joy at the right time. When the tale-tellers spoke, they used a great deal of eye contact. Hawaiians always say that that's how they know when you're not telling the truth—when you can't look them in the eye and talk. A storyteller is always judged for good eye contact. In other words, if I'm telling you the story, I look directly at you. You get the message. And there's always a message.

A storyteller is also a sort of teacher and preacher to the Hawaiian society. He is a teacher because he has to do research to get the specific information he needs. And then he preaches. Sometimes there's no existing story, but the tale-teller gets information, puts it together, and makes a new story out of it. This is done frequently. You combine the history and the traditional elements of story. The pronunciation of the Hawaiian words as well as English words must be very good.

Everything I've learned about story-telling, I have learned by watching someone else. I have watched many ministers. Some are good at delivering their sermons. They present the background first to set the stage. From there on, it's clear in your mind and the story can develop. I remember Father Thomas, a Catholic priest whom I adored as a child. I used to sit on his lap and listen to his stories by the hour. Once a month he would walk from Maunaloa to the east end, to do his visiting. He usually wore sandals on his feet, but sometimes he went barefooted. He had black garments and a black hat turned up on the side. He taught me a great deal about story-telling.

How did you relearn Hawaiian and teach yourself Molokai and Hawaiian history?

When I was president of Hui ʻImi Naʻauao, I used to conduct many classes on Hawaiian history. I got updated on where the Hawaiians came from and on the latest research about ancient navigation techniques and communication by researching in the Bishop Museum and the Archives and Dr. [Donald] Mitchell's book.

Introduction

From the end of World War II, when we had to travel on interisland boats, and for the next eighteen to twenty years, I studied, alone mostly, finally making my trips on the interisland planes. Dr. [Kenneth] Emory often came here to visit and taught me much. Mrs. Sophie Cooke of Molokai Ranch gave me access to the many places where others were forbidden to go. I already knew a lot about the east end, but I didn't know too much about the west end until I met Mrs. Cooke. We used to go bouncing all around the island in her jeep, so I could talk to old, old-timers like Koa Burrows, Sam Burrows, Joe Joao, and Dan Pahupu. After that, I conducted classes for the beginning teachers, teaching Hawaiiana.

At first I was a volunteer, then after awhile the government felt that I should be paid for teaching because I had made so many research trips to Honolulu. When I became historian for Molokai in 1964, the Lieutenant Governor's Office decided that if it sent anybody here to the island of Molokai, I would take them on tour and they would pay me. I took many people on tours, over the years, teaching them the history and telling them the stories of Molokai. It is the stories in this book that I used to tell them and my classes.

How did you come to be an ordained minister?

Well, my father was an ordained minister. During the early fifties, I went to Honolulu to visit him at his rectory. One night, as he was reading to me out of the Bible, he came to that scripture which talks about the harvest being great but the laborers being few. When he asked me if I was interested in the ministry, I told him I didn't feel qualified for it. He told me that all I had to do was give my heart to the Lord and study His words. I began to seriously study the Bible after that trip and to visit different churches to get different viewpoints from different pastors.

My friends had always come to me when they had personal needs, and I was able to help many of them. Through my prayers and my talking to the young people, folks thought that I had a true gift of

xi

ministering, and they had often told my father about it. For years my father kept telling me that maybe this was a God-given talent.

A couple years after that, I went again to Honolulu to visit him while he was having a Sunday school review. As I sat in the church there, I heard this voice calling me. Several times I went outdoors, even when it was raining, and then I ran back into the church. But before I ran back in, each time this voice would say, "Come, I need you." When I looked around, there was nobody there. I finally went back out when the rain stopped, but there was still nobody around, yet this time when I reentered the church, I had such a beautiful feeling inside that I cried. My father looked up and saw me crying.

Later I told him I felt beautiful and happy inside but at the same time sad, as if I were going to leave my present life and give up all that I had been doing. I somehow sensed I was going to live another life. He told me that this was my divine calling to the ministry and that I was resisting giving up my physical everyday life. When he saw that I was all mixed up, he suggested that we pray over it a couple of nights and then ask the Lord what was meant by this revelation.

I prayed for three days. Sometimes I felt happy, and sometimes I felt sad. One evening I went to a prayer meeting with a friend, and while there, I again heard this voice calling my name. Finally, I cried out loud without knowing what I was saying, "O Lord, I come, I come." Just then I heard the minister say, "When you hear the voice calling, you should not harden your heart but instead harken unto the call." At that moment, even though I knew it was a divine call to go into the ministry, I felt too young and unprepared.

When I went home I told my father about it, and he wanted me to go to a seminary on the mainland to study. I told him I would rather practice here in the islands, so he sent me on a novice training trip to the different islands. I spent one week on O'ahu, one week on Hawai'i, one week on Maui, and one week on Molokai. Every day I went out evangelizing into people's homes.

When I finally got back to Molokai, I went into our church and sat on the front pew. It was then this voice directed me to go up into the pulpit. I went halfway up, stopped, and sat on the step. The voice kept saying, "Go farther. Go on, up to the pulpit." But I returned to the bench, because I still didn't feel ready. Just then our neighbor's child came running in, grabbed my hand, and said, "Come, Auntie. Jesus told me to take you over there." I was amazed. Holding onto my hand, she tried to pull me up to the pulpit and onto the middle chair reserved for the pastor of the church. She then repeated, "Jesus told me to take you and sit you on the chair."

When I got home and told my husband about these events, he told me that he thought I was too young, but not to refuse the call of the Lord. He advised me that if I heard His voice again to go and tell my father that I had accepted the ministry. By then, my father was the bishop of the denomination.

The next morning early, this voice called me again and I quickly sat up in bed and said, "Yes?"

My husband woke up and said, "Nobody is calling you."

"Yes," I insisted, "a voice called me, distinctly by my full name, Harriet Ahiona Ne. It's the Lord calling me."

Right then and there I made up my mind. When my father came from Ho'olehua, he agreed to ordain me at the church on Molokai. The president of the denomination came, his secretary, and all the pastors of the different island churches.

All this was in the 1950s. Now I have been given the position of traveling pastor. Whenever the other pastors are sick or busy, they just send me to take over the pastorship. I go to different islands; but twice a month, I speak from the pulpit here at Kalama'ula on Molokai. They need me at the Kalama'ula church because I conduct some of the services in Hawaiian, including the sermons. There are children in that congregation now learning Hawaiian either at home or at school.

My experience as a *kupuna* and as a pastor embrace each other. My members address me as *Kahu*, meaning "Reverend." I often conduct *ho'oponopono* sessions, I mediate in local political affairs, try to bring families into harmony with one another, and teach Christian and Hawaiian principles of behavior.

It has been a pleasing life. In 1982, I went to Lā'ie to be honored as a "Na Mākua Māhalo 'Ia" (Give Thanks to the Elders). When I came back, Molokai High School had a special assembly, honoring me as an outstanding *kupuna* of Molokai.

Editor's note: Mrs. Ne died February 26, 1991, in Kaunakakai, Molokai, as this book was in the final stages of publication. She is survived by three brothers, Edward Manukula Ayau of O'ahu, Henry Keawe Ayau, Sr., of Ho'olehua, and Melvin Kealoha Ayau of California; her children, Anna Lu'ukia Arakaki, Reynolds Leialoha Ayau, Moana Kaulia, and Gerald Ne of Molokai, and Herbert Hooper of Japan; twenty-three grandchildren and eighteen great-grandchildren.

Those of us who felt her great spirit of aloha *have much to learn from her life and tales. She will be remembered.*

Tales
of the
Beginning

Hina,
the Mother of Molokai

In the very beginning, Hina gave birth to Molokai and watched over her beloved child.

Now, you will hear of several Hinas: the first Hina, the Moon Goddess; the second Hina, the Joan of Arc of Hawai'i; and the third Hina, the Mother of Molokai.

I will tell you a tale, a legend of the third Hina.

Very often she would come from her home in the sky to visit her child, Molokai. Down the rainbow she would glide until her feet touched the earth at Pelekunu. Immediately, raindrops the size of an infant's hand would fall thickly and heavily. In minutes the land was flooded with water.

The *kama'āina*s of old would say, *"Eia ka ua o Hina,"* which means, "Behold the rain of Hina." When the people of Pelekunu would see a rainbow touching their valley they would know that heavy rains were soon to fall.

In the sky could be seen the dark shadow of the goddess flying, arms outstretched and legs straight like a diver's. This dark shadow

would linger over Pelekunu and then move over to Wailau, to Moaʻula at Hālawa, to the plains of Moakea near Puʻu o Hōkū, and finally to the uplands of Moanui, flooding the land as she moved on. She would linger at Moanui, then move along the coastline to Honouli Wai, where she would again linger. At last she would drift out over the ocean to the coves where her favorite fish was available in abundance.

The *kamaʻāina* fishermen used to tell how they would be out on the rocks in the cove for hours and catch nothing. From the sun shining into the water, they could see deeply, deeply, but in all the dancing water they would see never a fish.

When the first raindrops fell on their faces, some of the fishermen would decide to go home. But those who knew the story of Hina would stay on with their nets ready to be cast into the sea, waiting, gazing into the water, seeing nothing. Though they would see nothing in the ocean, they believed what they had been told by their fathers and their fathers' fathers—that when the shadow of Hina covered them, they should quickly cast their nets into the sea anywhere near them, throwing blindly. And when the shadow finally disappeared from overhead, they should immediately begin to pull up their nets. It would take a long time because of the weight of the fish.

When they carried their catch ashore and opened their nets, they would be astonished and delighted because of the many *kala*, which we call surgeonfish. It was Hina's favorite fish. They were taught to take the best of the *kala* fish and put it on the *koʻa* for Hina. Anyone who failed to offer a *kala* fish to Hina would never again catch a fish in that cove.

After making their offering, the *kamaʻāina* fishermen would go home, whistling and sharing the fish with their neighbors. Then after the evening meal, the father would tell the story to his wife and children, who would all listen attentively, especially the sons.

They are long dead now, the sons of the sons of those sons. But who knows? It is said that Hina still visits the island in her mysterious way.

5

Ka'ohele,
the Hero of Molokai

As Pele is the legendary figure of the island of Hawai'i, and Māui is the legendary hero of the island of Maui, so Molokai also has its hero—Ka'ohele, the great runner, who could run from the east end to the west end of Molokai without tiring. Often he would run swiftly, straight from village to village, crossing streams and gullies without turning to the right or to the left, as he carried important messages for his chief.

He was born Ka'ohele Hulu at Kainalu on a bright moonlit night. At the moment of birth, he gave a loud wail, and immediately thunder roared from afar and a double rainbow appeared around the moon. The wise old men of the village marveled and affirmed that he would be a great man.

Yet as he grew up, Ka'ohele was a timid and gentle lad. He had a strong body and long legs but seemed to lack the fierce heart of a warrior. His parents taught him to fish, to carry wood for the family cooking, and to obey the village elders.

At the end of each day, it was the custom of the village to assemble all the youths and hold a footrace. The boy who won the race each evening returned to his home, picked up a cooking pot, and beat upon it mightily as a sign of his victory. Each year, at the *makahiki,* or fall festival of thanksgiving, peace, and games, the villagers came together for feasting and competitions. Kainalu had long been recognized for its many champions at racing, and all the boys in the village understood that the daily footrace was part of their training for this festival.

However, to the great disappointment of his parents, Ka'ohele was too shy to run in the evening races. His father became so angry that he threatened to send him away to live with relatives on the island of Hawai'i. His mother, afraid of losing him, encouraged him to train secretly at night. "I will teach you the secrets of becoming the fastest and strongest runner on the island," she promised.

Although Ka'ohele was shy, he wished to remain on Molokai, so he trained hard, running back and forth on the sandy shoreline, going over the same course again and again, his footsteps sinking deeper and deeper into the sand until he became exhausted and finally dropped onto the cool beach to rest.

His mother, an excellent teacher, taught him how to breathe, make fast starts, and maintain his speed. After each night of training, his mother massaged his leg muscles with *kukui*-nut oil to keep his muscles supple and flexible.

After three months of this secret and grueling training, Ka'ohele came to his father. "My father," he said shyly, with his eyes cast down, "I am ready to obey your wishes and enter the village races." His father was very pleased. When Ka'ohele made his appearance, the other villagers laughed and teased. He hesitated and almost turned away, but his mother whispered words of encouragement, urging him to compete.

When the signal was given to begin the race, Ka'ohele's strong legs carried him forward with enormous speed. All through the race he stayed ahead of the other runners. As was the custom, when he realized he had won the race he ran quickly to his home, picked up the first pan he could find, and began beating upon it to signal his victory. Tears of joy streamed down his face as he pounded the pan with pride and delight. News spread quickly through the village that the Hulu son had won the race. His parents hurried home, filled with pride and joy to share his victory.

The shy Ka'ohele loved to tease, especially his mother. So when she hugged him with excitement, he playfully rubbed soot on her nose from the victory pan. The pan he had picked to beat on was that in which his mother had cooked their morning taro, and his hand was black as night from beating upon it. His father clapped him on the shoulder and his mother composed a short victory song:

> *A kahi o'u*
> *Oi hā*
> *Pā 'ele, pā kini*
> *Pa'i na pō.*

> My first time
> With controlled breathing
> The black pan
> I struck, my hand turned dark as night.

Ka'ohele's pan song, sung to the tune of "Pease Porridge Hot," is still sung and played by the children of Molokai today.

After his first victory when he was but a lad, Ka'ohele was always the winner. He never failed to win the footraces during the *makahiki* games. Even the chiefs praised him for his agility, speed, and strength.

When Ka'ohele was twenty years old, the chief of Anahaki brought war against the chief of Pūko'o. Daringly, Ka'ohele stole into the village of Anahaki and brought out all the war spears. Although he was discovered and pursued, he was so swift and strong that he escaped, even carrying the spears. He dropped them at the feet of his chief in Pūko'o, then kept running to lead the warriors of Anahaki away from the village.

He led his pursuers up into the hills on the east end of Molokai, then down into the valley of Waialapa'i. Many miles later, he led them to Pu'u o Hōkū where he leaped a wide stream with ease. Even today, this place is known as Ka'ohele's Leap, and I myself have seen it. The Anahaki men spread up and down the bank, looking for a place to cross.

While they were thus engaged, Ka'ohele began to retrace his footsteps toward home at Kainalu. Realizing his strategy, the warriors of Anahaki raced toward Moanui to cut him off. Instantly, Ka'ohele ran into the gulch of Waialapa'i, now known as Pōhakupili, which would lead into the hills of Moakea and through which he could thread his way back to Kainalu.

His enemies were on the west ridge and, realizing that they could not get down fast enough to block him, rolled down a huge boulder to crush him. Ka'ohele, seeing their evil, loosed another boulder that stopped the first. And thus he escaped.

Even today in the gulch of Pōhakupili, you will find two large rocks, jammed against each other with a smaller rock wedged between. It is the site of Ka'ohele's heroic run and wise escape.

'Ōhi'a and the Birth
of Keala's Daughter

It was during the eleventh month, during 'Ikuwā, the season of thunderstorms and rough seas, that this adventure happened.

Keala and Kāwika were a young couple, Keala soon to give birth to their first child. They were happy and contented living at Kala'e Loa Harbor on the south coast of Molokai with all their hearts desired.

On this evening, they ate their fill and more of *poi*, fried mullet, and *'ulapapa*, or slipper lobster. They ate at leisure, with much talking and laughter. At last, they stretched and cleaned their hands.

"Kāwika," said Keala, smiling, "I long for a canoe ride on the ocean."

He shook his head. "This is not a good time. True, it is calm now, but the roaring winds and pounding surf of 'Ikuwā can come at any moment. In the harbor, it is tranquil and calm, but there will be heavy swells outside the point. Where do you want to go?"

"Eastward," said Keala with eagerness in her voice. "I hear that it is beautiful on that side of the island."

"We will go another time," said Kāwika. "If I were to require aid with the canoe, you might hurt yourself or the child in trying to help. Certainly, I do not want my child to be born at sea."

"Let it be so," said Keala laughing, "but promise me that we will go soon."

Not long afterward, during the third week of what is now November, on the night of the Mahealani Moon, Kāwika invited his fishing friend, Kuamu, to accompany them on a short trip. With anticipation, they prepared their nets and fishing gear while Keala prepared food and warm clothing. She was happy and laughed often as she did so.

When it came time to step into the canoe, Kāwika took her hand to help her into the canoe. At that moment, the baby in her belly kicked. Placing a hand on her belly, Keala said gently, "Be still, dear one. I am sure this voyage will be a pleasant one."

As they left the calmness in Kala'e Loa Harbor at Keawa Nui and headed east, Kāwika and Kuamu paddled hard and fast. Keala saw the next fishpond, which was called Pūhāloa, and spoke suddenly, "Turn into the cove before we come to Pūhāloa."

Kāwika was disturbed. "Such a thing is not for you to say, woman. It is for us to decide."

Despite his rough answer, Keala was not angry. "O husband, it is the words of the gods that I speak," she answered. "They have instructed me to direct this journey."

Kāwika was even more disturbed. "It is not the custom, woman. You are to repose yourself and be silent."

Keala turned away, wrapped herself in a *kīhei*, or tapa wrap, and settled herself at the bottom of the canoe.

Kuamu had not spoken, but he felt uneasy. "Kāwika, if the gods have spoken to Keala to direct us, then by all means let us turn into the cove." When Kāwika did not answer, Kuamu added slyly, "Is this not the cove where they make *moi li'i*, young *moi*, linger at this time of year?"

11

Kāwika allowed himself to be persuaded, and they turned into the cove. As they came closer to the shore, they saw schools of *moi li'i* near the sandy beach. Quickly they cast their nets and filled a section of the canoe with the little fish. Then Keala said, "Let us move on."

This time, Kāwika said nothing but took up his paddle. For the rest of the day, they paddled.

As night was falling, they came to another cove where Keala said, "Here we must turn in and beach the canoe. It is necessary that we share the fish with the people here. Then I must go to the *heiau* with some fish for my ancestors, the gods. We must make haste, for *moi li'i* are so tender they spoil easily."

"Rest in the canoe," said Kāwika to Keala. "Kuamu and I will take the fish to the village."

With laden baskets, they trotted off with the fish and were soon gone from sight. Keala could not rest, and instead lit a fire and began cooking some fish. Suddenly she heard a whining sound and looked up sharply. Firelight glinted on eyes in the circle of darkness, and she knew she had attracted a pack of *kupua*, or *mana* dogs. She threw them the cooked fish, feeling frightened and lonely. The baby kicked vigorously and she felt the first strong contraction.

Abandoning the fire, she went to the canoe and made herself as comfortable as she could. She was very hungry; and as if reading her mind, a *kupua* brought Keala a piece of the cooked fish. She took it gratefully and ate voraciously, but she was still not satisfied until she also took up some of the raw *moi li'i* in the canoe and ate them as well. The pack of *kupua*s surrounded the canoe, but she no longer felt afraid of them.

The contractions continued, and she knew that her child would be born that night. "I beg you," she spoke to the *kupua*s, "go to Hōkū-kano *heiau* and fetch my husband."

Howling and leaping, the *kupua*s disappeared into the darkness. In loneliness and fear, Keala began to weep. Just then, a man's voice

12

spoke kindly out of the darkness, "Why are you crying? Can I help you?"

Keala saw no one but answered without fear, "My baby will be born soon and there is no one to help me."

"I will bring help to you," said the man's voice. "Whom shall I bring?"

"I want my *kahu*, or nurse, Līloa, but she lives at Kala'e, many miles away," replied Keala.

"I will bring her," promised the man. Keala did not know that it was Ka'ohele, the fastest runner on Molokai, for whom darkness was no barrier.

Meanwhile, the *kupua*s had arrived at the Hōkūkano *heiau* and howled their message to the *kāhuna*. When they understood, they immediately began chanting, "May the gods keep the young woman in safety and ease her pain until help arrives."

Kāwika and Kuamu at once ran back to the canoe where they found Keala huddled, suffering greatly from the birth pangs. Kāwika helped her walk up and down the sandy beach, which greatly eased her.

When a light drizzle began to fall, Kāwika urged, "Let us return to the canoe where you will be dry."

"No," said Keala. "I feel better walking. Oh, how I wish my *kahu* were here."

Kāwika teased her, "You said you would give birth to your first child with no help at all."

Keala had no laughter for his teasing. "I did not know it would be like this," she whispered.

Just then, they heard a call, and out of the darkness leaped Ka'ohele with Līloa on his back. Amazed, the *kahu* said, "He has borne me all the way. He leaped over gullies and ran through ravines to find the shortest way. He is truly a *me'e*, or hero."

Keala greeted her with relief and Ka'ohele with gratitude, but there

13

was no time for speech. A loud peal of thunder sounded and the rain began to hiss down. Kāwika carried Keala into the canoe. With her *kīhei*, Kāwika and Kuamu made a shelter, bracing their backs against the lashing rain. The wind blew a gale, and the canoe rocked.

Suddenly, they heard the wail of the child. Līloa cried, "It is a daughter, O Kāwika."

Kāwika had wanted a son, but his disappointment disappeared in his joy at the birth. "What shall we name her?" he asked.

"Because she is so fat," joked Līloa, "let us call her Nuʻupē, 'Fat.' "

"No," said Keala. "Let us name her ʻŌhiʻakea, 'the Pale Mountain-Apple,' because she was born here where the stream from the ʻŌhiʻa Gulch empties into the sea, in the location where the gods directed us ashore."

The child was fair and Keala spoke the truth. Kāwika agreed with the name. And thus, a few days later, they returned in rejoicing to Kalaʻe Loa Harbor at Keawa Nui. As she held her daughter in her arms, Keala thought, "Some day we will return to ʻŌhiʻa and live there." And so it was.

14

Pueokea,
the Owl Daughter

It was long time ago when a beautiful daughter was born to a poor family in the village of Kawākiu Iki. They named her Pueokea and were very happy with their newborn child until dusk fell. Then, to their amazement, their daughter became a pale yellow owl.

The parents were fearful of the people of the village and took their daughter to a secret cave. During the day, her mother would slip quietly away to the cave to nurse and care for her child. She would take her daughter on her lap and rock her, chanting a lullaby while Pueokea fell asleep. Then she would wrap the child in her *pā'ū* and put her under a big rock where she would be warm. When dusk fell, the mother would leave with no fears for her daughter's safety, for at night the child became an owl and flew out to seek food and companionship with other owls.

On the day when Pueokea was one year old, her mother went to the cave with a beautiful yellow *pā'ū* which she had made for her, some baked sweet potato, and a beautiful wristlet of the kind for which their little village of Kawākiu Iki was known. Such wristlets were three inches wide and made of the mother-of-pearl that washed up on the beaches during the winter storms. The mother put this wristlet on Pueokea's arm, fed her some cooked fish and sweet potato, then put her to her breast and nursed her as she sang the weaning song: "You are grown, my child. This will be the last time you will suck my breast." Then she put the child on her lap and began chanting a lullaby.

This being a special day, she stayed longer than usual. Night came quickly; and suddenly Pueokea took the form of an owl, flapped her wings, and sprang from her mother's lap out of the cave. Her mother ran out to watch her fly southward, her eyes fastened to the light-colored shape until it faded out of sight. This was the last time she saw her child. She went to the cave daily but could not find her child. She even begged her husband to accompany her to the cave at night, but Pueokea never returned.

The mother bore six other children, three boys and three girls. They were all normal, healthy, and very handsome children. The parents loved them all, but the mother always yearned for her own beautiful Pueokea.

Twenty years went by. Then Pueokea's parents received an invitation to a *lū'au* in honor of the twentieth birthday of the chief's son from a new village just south of theirs. They were eager to meet this chief and see this new village, and gladly accepted.

The mother made a beautiful wristlet of mother-of-pearl to present as a gift. However, in her eagerness, she forgot her gift and did not remember it until they reached the *lū'au*. Her husband was very disturbed, for it was both ill luck and a breach of courtesy to present nothing at a birthday feast, especially to a chief's child.

Ashamed, they lingered in the background until almost everyone had eaten and were watching the chanting and dancing. As they took their humble places with those who had waited until the very end, a new group of dancers came out, all wearing red *pā'ū*s.

16

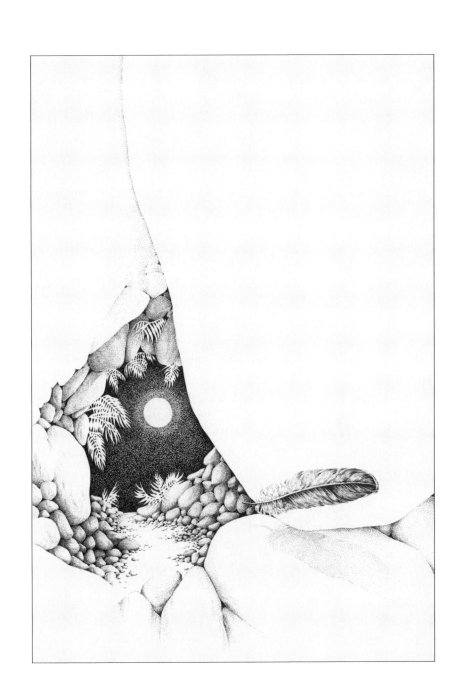

In the front line on the extreme right was a short, very fair and beautiful girl, wearing on her arm a wide mother-of-pearl wristlet. Instantly, the mother recognized it. It was the one she had made and given to Pueokea on her first birthday. Seizing her husband's arm, she whispered fiercely, "That is Pueokea, our lost child."

The father could not take his eyes from her, and they forgot to eat in their amazement. After that dance, the guests were introduced to the chief's son and presented their gifts. When Pueokea's parents were introduced, they hesitated to go forward until the guards seized them and brought them forth to be flogged for their discourtesy. When Pueokea saw this, she ran forward and offered her wristlet as a gift. Because Pueokea was so fair and beautiful, the chief's son added his pleas to hers. The chief forgave her parents, accepted her gift, and asked her to sit beside his son.

She accepted graciously; but as the shadows lengthened under the trees, she became ill at ease, turning away from the son's admiring eyes and forgetting to answer in the conversation. Her parents, too, were anxious.

When night fell, the chief's son had lost his heart and was holding her by the hand. To his amazement, her soft flesh and smooth skin suddenly became feathers. An owl rose before him and pecked his lips, crying mournfully, "I must leave now to meet my 'aumakua." He let go of her wing, and away she flew to the north.

Her parents watched her and knew that she was going home to Kawākiu Iki. With joy they prepared to follow her, but the chief's son detained them, pouring forth questions about Pueokea. They took pity on him and answered all his questions, telling him where he could find the secret cave. He left at once and went to the cave at dawn. There was Pueokea, curled up in her red *pā'ū* under a big rock. Around her head was wrapped a tiny yellow *pā'ū*, just the right size for a year-old daughter.

She greeted the chief's son with an exclamation of joy, and they were married soon after. Each time a child was born to them, a yellow owl appeared on the plains *mauka* of Kawākiu. It was *kapu* to kill an owl, especially a pale yellow one.

To this day, one who is driving along the highway to Maunaloa and to the hotel at Kepuhi may see an owl at night flying across the roadway. They have been known to be helpful to motorists stranded at night.

And I myself have seen them.

Puakea,
the Maiden of Molokai

This is a tale of long, long ago.

Puakea, a young and beautiful girl, wished for a home on Molokai. She had been born at Honokōhau on the island of Maui; but even as a young child, she would gaze across Pailolo Channel, tracing the outline of east Molokai with her yearning eyes and with a longing in her heart. Her father, Papa Piliwale, knew of this great desire in her heart and one summer day said to her, "Prepare yourself for a journey in a day or so. We shall cross the channel to Molokai and if we like what the island has to offer us, we shall plan to live there. Bring only the most needed things, for our canoe is not large and three passengers will not leave much room."

Speechless with excitement, Puakea immediately began to pack her most treasured belongings.

Papa Piliwale said, "We may all take a plant of our choice to remind us of our home here on Maui. I am going to take one or two stalks of *kō*, or sugarcane, and this variety we can use for medicine as well as for food."

Mama Piliwale said, "I plan to take the dried bean of the *'āwikiwiki* plant. You know how I love to eat the green bean. It also makes excellent medicine."

Puakea was undecided about what plant she wanted to take with her. Suddenly, her eyes lit on the *loulu lelo*, or fan palms, which had stood as sentinels in their yard for generations. Instantly she knew she would take the seeds of this tree, medicinal as well as decorative, to plant wherever they decided to make their new home. The seeds were light and could easily be rolled into her *pā'ū*. With this decision made, she called out, "I am ready."

Happily and with much anticipation, Puakea and her parents set sail out of Hāwea Point and charted their course for Pūko'o Harbor. The day was made for just such a happy journey, for the sky was blue and clear and the sea was calm as they paddled across the channel, singing as they went. Finally, in the late afternoon, they reached Pūko'o Harbor. As they gazed at the rolling hills and green gulches, they knew that this land was good and that they would build their new home to stand in the path of the tradewinds as they swept across the island.

"Let us unload our possessions and hide our canoe, and then we shall go on foot into this gulch," said Papa Piliwale, as he pointed to the north. They divided their loads evenly and walked until they reached a plain upon a hill. Here they made their home and later knew the vicinity was called Puna'ula.

Some time later, Puakea cut her foot on a sharp rock. In spite of all the loving care and the medicinal herbs prepared and applied by Papa Piliwale, the wound did not heal. The best medicine would have been from the sugarcane; but although the cuttings were growing well, it would be nearly a year before the cane was mature enough to use as effective medicine. Puakea was too ill to walk, and this made Papa very sad as he sat beside her trying to decide the best way to help her.

One evening Papa could hear the sound of the drums from 'Ili'ili'ōpae *heiau* drifting across the plain. Could this be an answer to his uncertainty? He carefully picked Puakea up in his arms and carried her to the *heiau* to visit the *kahuna* who was praying there. The *kahuna* laid his hands on Puakea and prayed. In a short while, the fever left her body. However, she continued to feel listless and weak and was not regaining her strength as quickly as she should; so Papa began to use the plants they had brought with them from Maui as medication for Puakea. In time she felt quite like her normal self.

During the time of Puakea's illness, Mama Piliwale had fallen ill. She was a very large woman and quiet, almost to the point of being withdrawn. Her illness clung to her and worsened each day. She refused to drink any of the medicines Papa Piliwale prepared but lay on the ground with her chin resting on her hands, staring in the direction of Maui, tears flowing down her cheeks.

Papa felt her sadness deeply. "Are you homesick?" he asked. "Do you wish to return to Maui?"

"No," she said, "I am going to die here. This is Puakea's home and she is happy here, but, oh, how I wish she would give us a *mo'opuna*. I want a grandchild."

In the meantime, Puakea's strength had returned fully, and with joy she took up the pattern of her daily life. Molokai was the home of her heart, for which she had yearned so long. She was welcome in the little community nearby and visited it daily, working with the women and playing with the young people.

One day as she was about to return home, a young man ran up to her, holding in his hand an *'awapuhi*, or wild ginger stalk. To her astonishment, he struck her on the head several times with it. It did not hurt and so, despite her amazement, she did not attempt to stop him. She was surrounded by a delightful fragrance; and when she put her hand to her head, she felt a silky substance on her hair. Puakea laughed and regarded the young man with pleasure.

"Come and rinse your hair in the fresh water," urged the young man. "You will be surprised at how good you feel and smell."

Puakea did as he said, then ran home to tell her parents of her unusual experience and to show them her fresh and fragrant hair.

"What was the name of the young man?" her mother asked, lifting the dark, delightful hair of her daughter in her hands.

"I do not know," Puakea replied. "It all happened too quickly, but I will find out soon what his name is."

The next day she hurried down the path to the village, and there, seated by the side of the footpath, was the young man. When he saw her, he smiled warmly. "*Aloha*," he greeted her.

"*Aloha*," answered Puakea. "What is your name?"

He answered her without hesitation, "If you wish, you may call me Pono as my friends and family do."

"I shall," she answered. "My name is Puakea."

"What a beautiful name!" Pono replied. "It is a name that suits you very well, for you are indeed a fair flower. I am afraid that I startled you yesterday. I hope that I did not hurt you?"

"Oh no," said Puakea. "You showed me something new and wonderful, and it gave me pleasure. I have told my parents about you. Will you come and meet them?"

"Gladly," said Pono, "but it is our custom here to welcome newcomers to the area with a gift, and I would like to take something to your family." He returned quickly with a bundle under his arm, and they set off down the path toward Puakea's home.

Mama and Papa saw them coming and greeted them as they came up the path. Pono presented his bundle, which turned out to be sweet potatoes, saying, "I planted these myself, and they have yielded well. I would like to share them with you."

"You have a good hand for planting," said Papa. "Would you help me plant the rest of the cane cuttings I brought with me from Maui? I want to be sure they will grow."

"Gladly," said Pono.

Together they planted the cane. Papa tied the sugarcane to *'ōhi'a 'ai* poles to keep the long stems from falling down. This was the first clump of sugarcane planted at Puna'ula to be supported by mountain-apple poles. When the cane took root and grew tall and straight in a clump, the villages called it *pu kō ko'o,* from "falling down" and "taking root."

And as the cane grew, so did the family take root in Molokai. Puakea and Pono fell in love and were married. When Mama Piliwale held her first *mo'opuna* in her arms, she knew she would live to see many more grandchildren that Puakea and Pono would give her. And it was so.

Kanalukaha and Hale o Lono,
Villages of the Two Brothers

O n the southwest coast of Molokai were the villages of Kanalukaha and Hale o Lono, settled in the ancient days by the Kepelino family. This is the tale of their founding.

One sunny day in Kona on the island of Hawai'i, Moke Kepelino spoke to his two sons, Kepa and Keao. "You must go to another island and find a place to settle and raise your families," he told them, "for they will need places for their own families." Kepa was a farmer and had four sons. Keao, a canoe-builder, was a fisherman and had three sons.

The brother of Moke, Moku'ohai, helped them build a large canoe. When it was completed, the family held a dedication ceremony and *lū'au* that was also an *aloha* for the departing sons. The *kahuna* blessed every part of the canoe. Then the men carried it into the ocean and dipped it in the water, then brought it ashore where the women filled it with two-finger *poi*. All of the happy people gathered round the *imu* and, when the pig was taken out, savory and steaming, took each one his or her portion, then took places at the canoe and dipped in.

It was a joyous occasion, and even the mothers of Kepa and Keao smiled, though their hearts were sad because they did not know when they would see their sons again.

The next morning, the men and boys loaded the canoe with taro plants, sugarcane cuttings, banana seedlings, and food and water for the trip. Then they boarded the canoe and paddled out until the current caught them and pushed them to Māʻalaea Bay on the island of Maui. The men went ashore and visited the area but decided they did not want to settle there.

So on they paddled. The ocean was very rough, till the wind behind their backs pushed them to a place of refuge at Keawa Nui, on shore at southeast Molokai. The people of a nearby village came to meet them; but their conversation seemed insincere and the Kepelino men decided they would move on.

They paddled on along the southern coast of Molokai until they turned up the southwestern shore. It was Kepa who saw a cliff with impressive black stones forming a large door or entrance to a cave. "Let's go ashore here," he told Keao. Pointing to a pile of rocks, he said, "I would like to build a temple for the worship of Lono on the face of that cliff."

So they beached the canoe on the shore and left their sons to watch it. The two brothers climbed up the cliff until they came to the black rocks and entered the cave. There was nothing in the cave, but as they emerged, they stood at the entrance admiring the ocean, beautiful and mysterious from that height.

"Shall we not stay here, brother?" asked Kepa.

"Yes," answered Keao, "and we can spend our first night here in this cave."

They joyfully ran down to the canoe and ordered the boys to carry their food up to the cave. At the mouth of the cave, they had their first meal on Molokai. They saw nothing and heard nothing of other people, and the sons wondered, "Is it an island unpeopled?"

Keao and Kepa were pleased. "We will establish our very own village here."

The next day, they walked inland to explore the area and find the water which was necessary before they could make a settlement and bring their women. Kepa and his sons went to the east, and Keao and his sons walked to the west. When Kepa saw a gulch leading northward, they followed it until they came to a *kukui*, or candlenut tree. They were very happy, since every part of this tree is useful. They continued walking and saw a large breadfruit tree, loaded with fruit.

Kepa's sons said, "Surely there is water nearby or this tree could never grow so green."

Kepa shook his head and pointed to the rainwater holes. "No," he said, "it is being watered by the rain." They continued to search, but they found no water.

Meanwhile, Keao and his sons had come upon a little spring under a great rock. They had discovered it when they noticed a flock of birds flying overhead, then diving down and coming up again.

"Search where they dive, my sons," he told them. "Perhaps it is water."

And so it was. When his sons ran to the spot, they saw water seeping out of the ground near a very large rock. Digging with their hands, they found the source.

Pleased and happy, Keao and his sons returned to the cave to bear the good news to Kepa and his sons. The next day, they returned with their stone tools, dug a larger hole, and watched the spring bubble up and fill the hole with water. Then they filled the hole with rocks. They drank the sweet, cool water and filled containers to carry back to the cave.

On their second night on Molokai, they ate a meal of dried fish and baked sweet potatoes, then stood at the mouth of the cave. Keao said, "This place shall be called Hale o Lono, 'House of Lono.' Tomorrow

27

we shall move out of the cave and consecrate it as a *heiau*, or shrine, for our family."

And so it was. The next day they arose early, filled a container with salt water, and consecrated the cave and the face of the cliff and called it Hale o Lono. On their third night, they slept on the shore at the base of the cliff.

On the fourth day, Kepa and his sons took the taro, sugarcane, and banana seedlings and went into the ravine to plant them near the water holes. They labored hard all day and finished just as the sun went down. Their last task was to build a little field *heiau* with a large rock. One of the sons of Kepa carved the image of Lono out of a *milo* trunk which he found in the gulch. Another son went to the bread-fruit tree to bring the choicest fruit for an offering, while the other sons went to bid Keao and his sons to this ceremony.

Kepa started with a prayer chant to honor Lono, the god of harvests, health, and weather. Then the offering ritual began with prayers and chants imploring Lono's blessings on the newly planted cane and seedlings. They made an offering of breadfruit and some *moi*, or threadfish, which Keao had caught just an hour before. After the peace offering, many prayers were offered promising that if Lono improved their crops, they would offer him products of the garden every night of the new moon. They returned to their camp on the beach with feelings of great happiness.

However, no sooner had they eaten their evening meal than Keao and Kepa got into a heated argument. Keao, the older of the two brothers, was jealous of Kepa. He felt that it would have been more fitting for him to hold the ceremony.

Kepa defended himself. "But it is I who am the farmer. It is for me to perform the blessing ceremony for planting."

Shocked and grieved, their sons intervened. "We have just prayed for peace and now you are fighting. Stop it or surely the god Lono will not answer our prayers." Their words were wise, and the two brothers asked each other for forgiveness.

The settlement went well. They brought their women and built their huts. Immediately and in harmony, Keao and his sons decided to build a fishing canoe. But where could they find a suitable log? Two by two, they set out on an even more prolonged exploration inland. On the fourth day, Keao came across an 'aiea tree large enough. He continued his search to locate stone from which they could make tools. Soon they found *uliuli*, suitable for making small adzes, and *ehuehu*, from which they could make axes.

Together, the men and boys set to work. After they completed the first axe, they held a ceremony, while one of the sons chopped the tree. Carrying the tree on their backs, they marched down to the sea chanting a ritual prayer. Already they had prepared a long pit near the shore with large stones on which to support the tree. This was their *hālau wa'a*, or canoe house.

The labor of shaping a canoe lasts for months. One day Keao threw up his hands in dismay. "*Auwē*," he said. "What are we going to use to seal the holes? There are no trees or shrubs we can use as sealer."

Kepa smiled, "Be easy, my brother. The sap from the breadfruit will make such a gum."

It was also Kepa who found, on the west side, some *kumuone*, or sandstone, with which to smooth the rough spots. The canoe was completed on *lā o Kū Lua*, about the second week in September. The ceremony of launching the canoe began early in the morning. The nine men and boys strained to lift the canoe into the ocean. They made but little progress, despite five attempts that bent their backs.

At that point, Keao said, "Wait, let me study the situation." He sat on the shore looking at the path they must take to reach the sea, through the soft sand. The waves were rolling halfway up the shore, but every fourth wave crested far past the others and came much higher, so high that it spilled wavelets into the pit where the canoe lay.

At that, Keao called the boys and said, "We will lift the canoe out of the pit on the fourth wave as it begins to return to the sea. Then we will push the canoe out with the help of the wave."

And that is how they launched the canoe.

They paddled five feet from the shore. Then Keao began the ritual of ocean launching by chanting a prayer to the god Kū. The prayer thanked Kū for helping them build the canoe in this place where material was so scarce. From the canoe, Keao swam to shore to build a *koʻa*, a fishing shrine, just north of the *hālau* on a stony outcropping with a shallow cave. Keao built his *koʻa* before the cave with a large black rock. Then he and his sons offered one small *moi*, one *kūmū*, one large *moi*, and some sugarcane to Kū. Then they paddled out to sea and came back at noon time. By catching the fourth wave, they brought the canoe with it exactly back into the pit.

Keao now turned to Kepa and said, "My brother, my sons and I will make our home here. We name this place Kanalukaha, 'the Fourth Wave.' Here we will worship Kū. You and your boys may live at Hale o Lono and worship your god, Lono."

So the brothers separated, Kepa to the gulch where he had planted his crops near the shrine to Lono, Keao to the site north of the *hālau waʻa*. The two families lived peacefully thereafter, sharing their crops and their fish catch like good brothers. Together they performed the ceremonies for good harvests and abundant fish catches.

As the sons grew older, they continued explorations inland and married women from Punākua, the nearest village. The population of Kanalukaha and Hale o Lono increased, but the villages are no longer there. When the families were too large for the amount of water, it became clear that some of the people would have to move—but so loving were they that they preferred to abandon their villages and move together to a new location than to separate.

And that is the story of the Kepelino brothers.

Tales
of
Naming

Kamalō,
the Taro Patch Pool

This is the tale of the naming of Kamalō, "the Pool of the Taro Patch."

In the early days of our island, Kamalō was known as Kamalo'o, "the Dry Place," because this was where the sea dried up and the waves, breaking outside on the reef, did not come up to the shore. The people of Kamalo'o liked such shallow beach pools, for they were beloved of the squid, and nothing could have pleased the people more.

A *kama'āina* named Jack Ka'ilianu one day observed to the others, "We have an abundant supply of food from the sea. Why should we not make it sure and make fish farms in our pools?"

This pleased the fishermen and together they made *loko wai*, or freshwater ponds, where the streams ran down to the shore. Others built *pu'uone*, or sand-dune ponds, by digging an inlet from the sea to the pond, scooping the wet sand into banks, and stamping it down firmly to make them hard. These brackish ponds were naturally less complicated to build, for the *loko wai* were built very much as the people made *lo'i kalo*, or terraces for taro patches—making banks with mud, dry leaves, small twigs, and pebbles and stamping them down hard so that the water would not drain out too fast. It was a lot of work.

In the *pu'uone*, the fishermen accumulated their stock of *pua*, or young fish. The type of fish that thrived in these ponds were *pua 'ama'ama*, or mullet; *pua awa*, or milkfish; *kūmū*, or goatfish, and *mao*. Many people raised fish like pigs and even made pets of them. They would catch the fish in their hands. The fish fed on the algae in the ponds and were given cooked taro peelings.

Jack Ka'ilianu wanted to be different, since his taro patches were very close to the sea. He decided to use his taro patch as a fishpond too. He put *pua āholehole*, *pua awa*, and *pua 'ama'ama* into his *loko-lo'i kalo*, or taro pond. His fish thrived and grew fast. Jack discovered that their stirring about and feeding helped to keep the water fresh. The mullets thrived in the liquid mud and the taro grew tall and yielded a good harvest.

Jack had a fourteen-year-old *hānai* son named Puni, whom he asked to tend the *lokolo'i kalo* in addition to his other chore of tending the sweet potato patch. Puni was very happy to do so because he loved to watch the fish swim around the pond.

It was because of his fondness for fish that he caused trouble for his father. One day he caught many small *'iao* fish, or silversides, and released them in the taro pond. *'Iao* are used as bait in fishing for *aku*, and they resemble lizards. Now, the *'aumakua*, or guardian god, of Kamalo'o was the *mo'o*, or lizard, so it was *kapu* to kill a lizard of any sort. Since the *'iao* fish look just like lizards, it was *kapu* to catch them or eat them too.

It was many weeks before Jack went to the pond and saw the *'iao*. Angrily, he called Puni. "You have done a great wrong. You have broken the *kapu*," he scolded him. "You must catch all of the *'iao* and put them back in the ocean."

34

Puni did not obey, because he had made pets of the little fishes. Every day as he approached the pond he would pound the bank, and all the *'iao* would swim towards him. He would lie on his stomach and put his hand, covered with mashed taro, into the water. Greedily, the *'iao* would eat the taro particles from his fingers, tickling the tender skin of his fingers and between his fingers. He would giggle and squirm. In his pleasure over the *'iao*, he did not want to return them to the ocean.

When Jack discovered that Puni had disobeyed him, he went himself, caught the *'iao*, and released them in the ocean. The next day, Puni did not come home for the evening meal.

Jack searched all the village, calling for him. At last, he went to the *lokolo'i kalo*. What did he see? In horror, he perceived Puni's body floating in the pond with many little fishes swimming around his ears and nose. In the palm of his hand were some *'iao* that Jack had not been able to catch.

The people of the village truly mourned for Puni. He was well loved by all. Every time Jack looked out at the ponds, he recalled the reason for them and muttered under his breath, *"Kamalo'o kā kā 'āina"* (The land has gone dry. It is no longer verdant).

Brokenhearted, he exchanged the pond for a piece of land further upland, abandoning the taro in the pond to wither and die unattended.

And for many years after, the people could hear the giggling of a child coming up from that pond.

Pu'u o Hōkū,
the Hill of Stars

This is the tale of the naming of Pu'u o Hōkū, "the Hill of Stars."
Nakoa was a lonely man, who lived by himself and seldom spoke,
not even to his neighbors, the people of Pa'uwela on Maui. He had a
dark reason for his silence. A chief from Kukuihaele was seeking him
for breaking a serious *kapu,* and Nakoa lived in constant fear of being
captured and killed.

One night he dreamed a dream in which a voice spoke, "Gaze
always over the bays of Pi'ilani." He began to do so, and his neighbors thought him even stranger than before. But one day, he saw a
white cloud shaped like a finger pointing to Molokai. At once he recognized it as a sign, took his canoe, and paddled under the cloud,
going in the direction the finger pointed. After four hours of steady
paddling, he landed on the beach at Kāhei Point.

He beached his canoe and stood on the shore watching the finger
cloud. He was amazed to see the finger point upward and thought to
himself, I certainly can't go up into the sky. What is the sign saying?
Perhaps it is telling me to climb the cliff and go upland?

Wasting no time, he began to climb the cliff. But when he got to the top he saw another hill and another. After he had climbed three hills, it was nightfall.

Exhausted, he sat down, then lay on his back and gazed in the sky. Suddenly he had a glorious feeling as if he could reach up and touch the stars. "I shall call this place Puʻu o Hōkū, or 'Hill of the Stars,' " he whispered. He did not move and finally fell fast asleep, his eyes closing as he still gazed at the stars.

He awoke the next day and went to see the famed *kahuna* Lanikāula of the sacred *kukui* grove. He told Lanikāula of his life of fear and confessed his fault in breaking the *kapu.*

"You need not run any more," Lanikāula told him. "It is the will of the gods that you stay here at Puʻu o Hōkū. You will always be safe here."

Thus it was that Nakoa lived on the Hill of the Stars till the end of his days, lonely no longer.

Ka Lae o ka Lā'au, the Point of the Branch

This is the tale of the naming of Ka Lae o ka Lā'au, "the Point of the Branch."

It was long ago, two hundred years ago, when the shark god of Kainalu left his home off Molokai and traveled to Kaua'i. Where the Wailua River spilled into the sea, he lingered and romped in the ocean until he was joined by the shark god of Kaua'i.

Floating in the sea was a large branch of the *hau* tree, and in their play, it became stuck on the back of the Molokai shark. Despite his efforts, he could not shake it off. At last, he ceased writhing and twisting and swam quickly toward Molokai. There, off the southwest point, the *hau* branch came loose and was washed ashore.

The people on the beach saw it float ashore. A week before, they had seen two ships cruising offshore, the first they had ever seen. They had admired the vessels and said, "Surely the branch is a gift from the strange canoes." They took the branch and carried it inland to a fertile bit of land where some wild *'ilima* grew. There they planted it. Their chief, Kuamu, said, "We shall call this place Ka Lae o ka Lā'au, or 'the Point of the Branch.' "

On that point, the land is very dry and arid with hardly any vegetation, but the *hau* took root. It is not like the Hawaiian variety. Its leaves are smaller, and it has many small seeds. It is short and sprawls close to the earth, bending like a vine before the winds; but its blossoms are beautiful, so beautiful that the people of Molokai offered them to their gods.

It grows there to this day and I myself have seen it.

The Red Dog
of 'Īlio Point

This is the tale of the naming of Ka Lae o ka 'Īlio, or "the Point of the Dog."

In ancient times, the *kama'āina*s believed that each region by the sea was watched over by a shark god. The shark god of Kainalu had an ancestor whose bones washed ashore on the northwest end of Molokai, and the people there gathered the bones and made a shrine.

When the Kainalu shark wished to pay his respects to his dead ancestor, he could not go by water. He could not swim there and back between sunset and sunrise; and during the day, the shark gods of the other areas would be about. They knew that it was *kapu* for him to go beyond his own district, and his punishment would be great if he were caught violating this prohibition.

And so he found his solution this way. His mother was a dog worshiper, so he went on land and took the form of a dog. Every fifth year, he trotted to his ancestor's shrine at 'Īlio Point, did homage, and then slipped into the sea where he took his own form and returned during the night while the other shark gods slept.

41

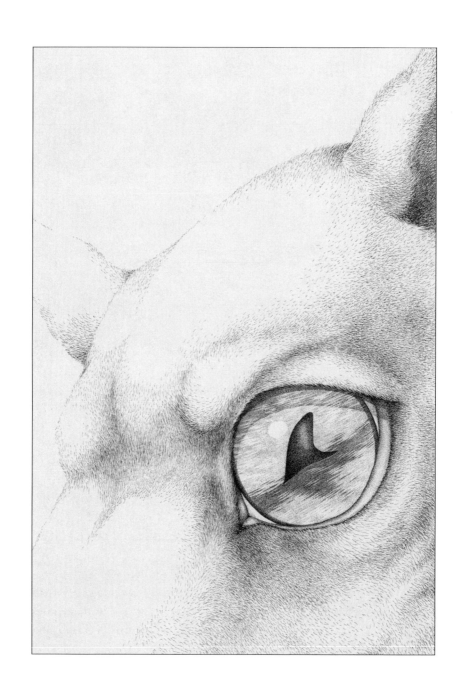

The Red Dog

Many people have seen him. Some call him the Red Dog because of his color, and others call him the Sausage Dog, because he can make his body long like a shark's.

I myself have seen this long red dog sniffing along the roadside toward the northwest point of Molokai. There I have seen him sniff about the *heiau,* stand on a large slab of stone, and lift his head to howl. Then I have seen him walk into the ocean and disappear. And surely he will return.

Ka Lae o ka Manu,
the Point of the Birds

This is the tale of the naming of Ka Lae o ka Manu, or "the Point of the Birds," during the days of Kamehameha V.

From Tahiti they came, the *kōlea* birds, forty of them flying in a single flock, and four flocks that came, one after the other. First they alighted on the island of Kaua'i, but it did not please them, so they flew to O'ahu. Some of them stayed on O'ahu, but the rest came to Molokai.

They were exhausted by their long flight and settled down on this point, on a sand spit in front of Malama at Kaunakakai, feeding on a kind of small red bird that is faintly flavored with salt. And so they stayed, giving their name to this point.

Pāpōhaku,
the Stone Wall

This is the tale of the naming of Pāpōhaku, or "the Stone Wall."

In ancient times, a chief from east Molokai and a few of his people boarded canoes and set off around the island. When they came to the southwest coast of Molokai, they paddled up to some fishermen who had a large catch of 'ōpelu, or mackerel scad. Willingly, they shared the catch with the strangers.

The chief was very hungry and ordered his men to prepare a meal of raw fish and *poi.* Soon they were all eating with great satisfaction; but in the middle of their meal, another group of fishermen came by and cried, "Stop. Do not eat the 'ōpelu. This is the season of 'ōpelu *kapu.*" The village of the chief had only a *kapu* for eating turtle, so they continued their meal.

The fishermen on the other canoe were mad with outrage and fear. They attacked the chief and his men, overpowered them, and hauled them ashore. There they brought the strangers before the *kahuna.*

The *kahuna* explained to the strangers that at this village certain

45

kinds of fish were *kapu* to chiefs, and at this particular time *'ōpelu* was *kapu*. The chief became very ill. The *kahuna* conducted many ceremonies and rituals to correct this error, but they were of no avail. Only a human sacrifice could make things right with the gods and save the chief from death.

One of his men offered himself as a sacrifice, and so it was done. The chief recovered. Then the *kahuna* ordered a tree planted on the grave of the willing victim.

The grave was on the shore; when the tide was high, the waves would wash sand from the grave. Thus, in a very short time, the body would be exposed.

In respect and remembrance, the chief ordered his men to build a stone wall about fifty feet long. They worked with great diligence, their hearts full of gratitude for the willingness of their fellow to die in the chief's place, and their work was beautiful. The chief then ordered them to continue building the wall for another two hundred feet. The chief himself put the last stone on the wall, saying as he did so, "I call this place Pāpōhaku, 'Stone Wall.' "

The stone wall still stands today, marking off a long stretch of the white sand beach, Pāpōhaku.

I myself have seen it.

Hālena,
the Yellowing

This is the tale of the naming of Hālena, which means "yellow."

When Kahekili was the ruling chief of Molokai, he lived on Maui. He made his plans and set out in his canoes to invade Oʻahu, stopping at Molokai to get a supply of fish for his journey. He sent Hulu, chief of a village, in his canoe to Pūkoʻo for the fat mullet from the fishponds. He sent another canoe with another chief, Kuikai, to Pālāʻau, noted for its fat *āholehole* and *ʻōʻio.*

Meanwhile, Kahekili and his men paddled on to the southwest. As he looked ashore, he saw no taro patches or people, nor did the land look fertile; but he knew that he must find drinking water for his men. Just as the sun was sinking, he chose the most promising stretch of coastline, and they beached their canoes. Kahekili sent his men to explore the land.

As he himself searched for signs of life, he heard the wail of a newborn child and sent his men to investigate. They discovered a large cave containing several people, including a woman with newborn babe.

47

They related this information to Kahekili, who sent one of the men to his canoe to fetch a bundle amongst his personal belongings. With dignity, the great chief entered the cave and presented himself before the infant. The people recognized him as an *ali'i nui* from the symbols on his cape and bowed before him, while the chief of the district, the father of the infant, welcomed him according to royal traditions and introduced his wife and baby son.

Kahekili unwrapped the bundle and took out a piece of white tapa cloth as his gift to the newborn son of a lesser chief. As was the custom, he breathed upon the tapa, then gave it to the lesser chief, who, in turn, breathed on it. As he did so, the white tapa turned yellow, a sign that he was sickly.

The lesser chief offered the hospitality of his cave to Kahekili and his men for the night. Kahekili accepted with thanks, and the people immediately prepared a meal for them. After eating, they all retired, for they were very tired from their long journey.

The next morning, the lesser chief asked timidly, "Why did you stop here if you were going to O'ahu?"

Kahekili replied, "We stopped here to get a supply of fish for our journey. Your hospitality has been most welcome, and we thank you. What is the name of this place?"

"There is no name for this place," said the lesser chief.

Kahekili responded, "Then I shall call it Hālena because of the sign of the yellowish tapa."

And so it was.

Pe'elua Hill

Up at Ho'olehua by the old Latter-day Saint chapel is a hill which is called Pu'u Kape'elua, or "Caterpillar Hill." It is strewn with many great boulders; and underneath one boulder is a large, round indentation. Now the caterpillar is the *'aumakua* of that district, and this is the story of the naming of that hill.

A beautiful young girl named Pele, the daughter of a chief in the Pālā'au area, encountered in the early twilight a handsome young man. They fell in love, and he courted her for almost a year. She concealed her love from her parents and lived only for the hours she spent with him.

She did not know that he was the *pe'elua* of the district, revered and loved by the people of Ho'olehua—even worshiped. Nor did she know that he had the form of a young man only at night but that in the day he returned to the form of a caterpillar.

As the days passed, Pele grew pale and listless. It was her old nurse who came to Pele's father and said, "Look at your daughter. She looks sick. She has no strength. Her face is pale and her eyes are heavy."

The chief looked at his daughter attentively and saw that it was so. "She looks drained. We must tell her mother," he said.

When the mother saw her child's illness, she said at once, "We must take her to the *kahuna*."

The *kahuna* perceived the problem at once. "She is in love with the supreme manifestation of the caterpillar—Pe'elua," he told them. "When he comes to her at night, it is in the form of a handsome young man; but his power is draining her strength. She is human. She cannot live with a magical being. To save her, you must kill him. You must destroy him completely."

Her parents were astonished and frightened, for they had known nothing of her lover. "We do not know this young man. We do not know where to find him," they said.

The *kahuna* advised them, "Tell your daughter everything. Tell her that she will die if he is not killed. She must make it possible for you to find him."

When the parents spoke to Pele, she wept in anguish. "What can be done? Why must he be destroyed?"

But her father ordered, "Tear off a piece of your tapa and fasten it to his tail so that we can follow him."

At last she agreed.

That night, the young man came as usual. When he fell asleep near her, she tore off a piece of her tapa and tied it to his back.

The next morning he woke in the early dawn, very near the time that he would again become a caterpillar. Frightened at the lateness, he ran quickly up the hill toward Ho'olehua. The father, the *kahuna*, and some of the men followed him until his footsteps disappeared, but they found traces on the earth as if something broad had swept it. Then they knew he had again become a caterpillar but that the tapa was brushing the earth.

They followed these traces to the hill by Ho'olehua and tracked it between the great boulders. Under a huge stone, they found the caterpillar, curled up in sleep.

They looked to the *kahuna* for guidance. He did not waver or draw back from the task. "Now we must gather all the sticks and dried leaves we can find," he ordered. "We must pile them on top of him and set them alight."

They all obeyed him. The caterpillar did not awaken as they covered him with the twigs and sticks; but when they struck the match and ignited the fire, he burst into a million caterpillars.

And that is why the Ho'olehua people have all of the caterpillars on Molokai.

Tales
of
Long Ago

The Attack of the
Three Hundred Canoes

Before Kamehameha I conquered the islands, Molokai was threatened by the king of Maui, who greatly desired it. From Maui, he saw Molokai looking green and fertile, not realizing that he was deceived by the light and distance. So it was that he made his plans and launched his war canoes, three hundred of them lined up along the shore.

But one of the chiefs from the east end of Molokai was aware of these plans and had warned all the other chiefs to be prepared. In a council of chiefs, he explained, "In the past, all wars on all the islands have been fought with spears, and the victory has gone to the strongest in close work. Listen to me, O chiefs, and do not make spears but arm your people with slings."

So they gathered highly polished stones, hard, hard like marble. I myself have one of these stones that has come down from one generation to the next until it has reached my hands. Women and children and young boys and girls made piles and piles of those stones, and

with every stone came new determination that it would repel an enemy. And then each warrior made a sling for himself, laboring over the wood and thongs, and casting stones at marks small and far away until they were perfect in their aim.

Thus, when the Maui king arrived, the Molokai warriors were prepared, concealed behind the stones and the brush on the hillside that sloped down to the sea, lying flat and still in places where there was no cover, for the hill was too dry for trees.

Quickly the warriors of Maui leaped from their canoes. Quickly they came forward, their spears poised to throw. Quickly they began to climb the hillside toward the ridge. Silently waited the warriors of Molokai. When the first men of Maui saw movement on the ridge, they cried out and threw their spears; but they were too eager and had thrown too soon. Their spears fell short. As they ran forward, still waited the men of Molokai. Then at the word of command, they rose up with their slings and their smooth, hard stones. It was a harvest of death as they flung their stones and slew their enemies, heaping their bodies all down the hillside to the canoes.

Those few who were still alive ran back down the slope, the deadly whistle of the stones in their ears, and met their king as he prepared to beach his canoe. In an instant he saw the work of death. At once, they climbed, bruised and bleeding, into canoes and paddled for the open sea. And thus it was that the warriors of Molokai repelled the invasion from Maui.

Auwē, auwē.

The War Strategy
of Kamehameha I

When Kamehameha I set about conquering Molokai, he came not with war canoes and spears but softly and shrewdly. With his wisest counselors, he came to the east end, greeted the chiefs and the people peaceably, and sat in council with them. It was his offer to teach the warriors of Molokai the tactics and strategies of war that he had used on the island of Hawai'i and the island of Maui.

Haughtily the chiefs of the central highlands invited him to train their warriors, and humbly Kamehameha came, teaching the warriors for almost two years. But when the two years were over, he knew the island, he knew the chiefs, he knew the strengths and weaknesses of their army—and he had reserved his finest strategy as a secret.

He then went back to Maui to live, and the warriors he left in Molokai were placed under different chiefs in different districts where each chief used a different strategy. All Kamehameha knew was of no use, for he was shocked when they fought differently from his teaching!

So it was that he lost many battles, here on Molokai. But the people loved him and they submitted to him. They allowed him to bring Molokai under his rule in 1792, and thus Molokai also became part of his united Hawaiian kingdom.

Kepuhi,
Village of the Eel

Kepuhi was but a small village in Kaluako'i on west Molokai, ruled for many generations by the Nu'uhiwa family. Their last chief was named Lono Nu'uhiwa. On his sixtieth birthday, the entire village celebrated the happy occasion with him in a great feast. However, despite the celebration, the chief's heart was heavy. He realized that he was getting old and had no sons. If he died without naming a successor the *kahuna* would rule the village, but he was a dreamy man, not a leader.

With great attentiveness, he began to study the young men of the village. His favor fell upon a young man named Keao. Keao was a fish spotter. Every morning he would climb the high stones to look out into the ocean. His keen eye could see below the glancing surface to see patterns in the waves and the dives of sea birds which meant that schools of fish swam beneath the waters. Accurately, he would signal the fishermen, who would take their boats out and bring back good catches.

Keao was a slim, handsome young man, but he was also very shy. The chief loved him like a son; but as he thought about the qualities of a chief, he knew that Keao was too amiable, too gentle and withdrawn. He had said nothing to anyone about Keao and, with regret, he cast his eye elsewhere.

So matters stood on the day that Keao, from his tall rock, saw a large object floating in the ocean. He watched until it drifted closer. It was a canoe, and in it lay the body of a beautiful girl. He plunged into the waves and brought it up on the sandy beach. The girl was unconscious, and Keao's efforts to revive her failed. He picked her up in his arms and carried her to the chief's house, gazing upon her lovely face. With each step, he fell more deeply in love with her.

When the girl awoke, the chief asked her name. "My name is Auhea," she replied. "I live at Makapu'u on O'ahu." After they had cared for her and given her food and water, she told them her story. She was fishing with her brother when they were attacked by a large eel at Makapu'u. She had only enough strength to swim to their canoe and climb aboard before losing consciousness.

The chief wondered at her story, for the 'aumakua, or guardian god, of Kepuhi was a giant moray eel. No one in the village was allowed to kill or eat eel. What could it mean that an eel had been responsible for the arrival of this woman in his village?

Auhea, weak from her suffering, wept as she thought of her brother. Raising her eyes, they fell on the face of Keao, whose own eyes had never left her face; and in them she saw comfort for her loneliness.

Auhea stayed with the chief for a month. During this time, she responded to the love of Keao and fell deeply in love with him. When he asked her to marry him, she accepted with gladness and became his bride with joy. Auhea was happy at Kepuhi and made no attempt to return to her village. When she became pregnant, the village rejoiced; but it was a particular happiness to the chief.

One night the *kahuna* dreamed that the chief of the village to suc-

61

ceed Lono would have the mark of the eel on his body. Lono felt the truthfulness of this dream; but within a few nights, he died, naming no successor. The people, in grief and distress, did not know what to do, but the *kahuna nui* comforted them, "One day soon we will learn who is to be the next chief of Kepuhi."

Three months later Auhea gave birth to a husky boy. On the day appointed for the dedication of the baby, all the people assembled at the *heiau*. As Auhea lifted the baby to the *kahuna*, he saw three white marks running down the right side of the baby's face from his ear to his mouth. Instantly, the *kahuna* broke into a joyful chant: "Behold the mark of the eel. Behold the high chief of Kepuhi."

For days the villagers celebrated the event, and the baby became a noble and wise chief.

Even to this day, the giant moray eel lies quietly on the reef near the blocks of limestone. It has never been known to attack a person. The only time the eel uncurls and swims in the pools of water on the reef is when the *kama'āina*s come to feed him small fishes. After eating their offerings, he slides among the rocks to a secluded spot and settles down once again into a contented curl.

And so life was lived, in harmony and balance, in the village of Kepuhi.

The Phallic Rock
of Nānāhoa

If you pass through Kualapu'u to the forest, you can see the great rock six feet high which is called Kaule o Nānāhoa, which means "the penis of Nānāhoa." Nānāhoa was a prince who lived on the Twin Hill and protected the rock because it was on his property. Also, it was precious to his people because it was known to cure infertility.

But for him—and not only for him—it was a sorrow.

He was married to a beautiful woman, and they were very happy until another woman came from another district. Nānāhoa did not resist her loving glances, and soon they became lovers. The heart of his wife burned hotly within her; and when she found them together at the rock, she cried out in rage and hurled bitter accusations at them.

Then she sprang at the woman and pushed her down the cliff. Even today, if you go there, you will find a perfectly formed female rock.

I myself have seen it.

The Talking Shell

In Anahaki beyond Ho'olehua on the ocean side in the ancient days, they trained warriors for battle. The chief was a kindly man, well loved by his people and greatly respected, for he could prophesy the future. He could tell whether an enemy from another village was plotting an attack, or whether there would be no fish in the ocean, or when the turtles would come. He could warn the people of an approaching famine and console them with the promise of the rain. And he was never wrong. Whatever he prophesied came to pass.

One of the young warriors being trained by this chief craved his power. He wanted to be the next chief of the village, but he was not of the chief's family and knew that the consideration of the village would never fall upon him unless he could perform an extraordinary feat. Then, despite his lineage, the voice of the people would speak for him, making him chief. He yearned for the prophetic gift of the chief and thought in his heart, It is possible for a man to guess where the turtles might be or when the rains might come, but it is impossible

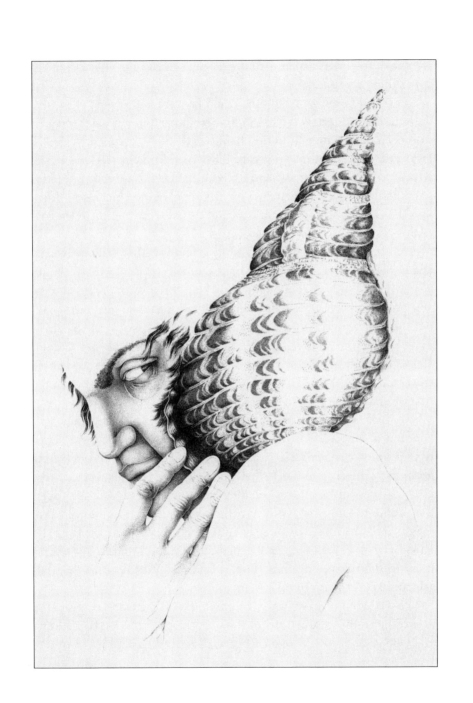

for a man to guess correctly all the time. How can the chief prophesy correctly every time?

So he set himself to watch the chief day and night. And then, one dark midnight, he saw the chief come from his hut and walk towards the ocean. Creeping within the shadows, the young warrior followed him. The chief went into a great hollow within the rocks like a cave where the ocean water swelled up with the tide. The young warrior knew that cavern and watched from hiding as the chief went down into the cave, working his way around the edge of the tide to the side of this cave where a shelf of rock jutted out.

From that shelf, the chief picked up a large shell. The warrior also knew the shelf and the shell. He had seen them there for many, many years, but he had never thought to pick up the shell. Now he saw the chief hold the shell in his hands, lifting it to his ear. He saw him speak, but the roar and hiss of the tide drowned out the words of the chief. Then he saw the chief replace the shell on the shelf and speak again. This time the warrior could see from the movement of his lips that the chief said, "*Māhalo*" (Thank you). As the warrior watched from the shadows, the chief returned to his *hale*.

The next day, the chief summoned the people together and announced that warriors from the east planned to attack them. They were jealous of the good location of the village near the fertile fishing grounds of both fish and turtles and wanted freedom to reach the ocean as they wished, for when they had come before, as was proper, they came to the chief, told him their errand, and announced that they would only stay for three or four days. As was proper, the chief had always greeted them on behalf of the village and had welcomed them to the fishing grounds. But he had also noticed that they left reluctantly and grudged their thanks.

The warriors of the village, including the young warrior, prepared according to the instructions of the war chief, who selected a hiding place behind an old crooked stone wall and instructed them to pile stones for their slings there. He ordered, "When we see them coming, do not throw the stones until I give you the command. We must wait until they approach within thirty feet so that we can aim with the best effect."

The young warrior prepared stones with the others. With the others, he crouched there that night. And with the others, he was roused at about three o'clock in the morning when they saw the dark figures creeping toward the village. Like the others, he fitted his stone to his sling.

The war chief said, "Wait! . . . not yet . . . not yet. . . ." With his voice he held them as they tensed, their slings in their hands.

"Wait still," he murmured.

And still they waited, until the eastern warriors had come within thirty feet, moving soundlessly over the sand.

With his command, the war chief released his warriors to fight. With a shout, they rose up, their slings whirring in their hands, releasing the stones of death at the enemy. Their aim was good. Every enemy that came within thirty feet fell instantly. With spears, the warriors passed among them, killing those that were still alive and driving the enemy back with great slaughter.

The young warrior was among them. Like the others he had waited, risen, cast his stone, and pursued with his spear. Like the others he rejoiced in the victory celebration that followed. But all the time, his mind was busy with the memory of the chief, holding to his ear the shell in the cavern.

That night, while the village slept, the young warrior watched again. Again he crouched in the shadows. Again he saw the chief emerge from his *hale.* This time he ran ahead of the chief, running like a shadow within shadows and hiding within the shadows of the cavern so that he could be close enough to hear.

In a few minutes, he heard the chief come into the cavern and find his way to the shelf. He heard the chief say, "Forgive me, for I am listening to what you say." Again the chief held the shell to his ear, but this time he said nothing more until he replaced it on the shelf and again said, "*Māhalo*."

The next day, the chief told the village, "We have a man right within our own camp who wants to be chief. He must be stopped for he wishes the chiefdom only for its power."

The young warrior felt fear come upon him, but he spoke no word. Within him he was still determined to become chief. That night, as soon as the village was asleep, he went to the cavern of the shell, picked it up, and inclined his ear to it. All he heard was the washing and roaring of the ocean. Then he said, "Speak, that I may hear your wise sayings."

Then a voice spoke, telling him that the villagers should leave their village and go to Pipika because the spring of Anahaki was going to be dry for a week or more.

The young man returned to the village. Next day, he listened as the chief came forth from his *hale*, but he had a troubled countenance and gave no message to the village. Thus, the young warrior knew that the shell spoke its message only once. He also knew that he could no longer stay in the village.

To his family, he said, "Let us go to Pipika."

The family was puzzled by his speech and asked, "Why?"

"The spring is going to dry up, and there will be no water."

His grandmother looked upon him steadfastly and said, "No, no. I do not believe you. The spring of Anahaki has given us its water for years and years. Is there not a promise that this spring will never run dry? And would not the chief warn us?"

The warrior's father and mother, looking upon him, said, "We will go with you and bring the other children," but his grandmother said, "No! I was born in this village, I will die in this village."

As they prepared to leave, many of the villagers came, among them the chief. "Where you going?" the chief asked.

The young warrior, speaking for his father, said, "Oh, we are going to move. We going up to Pipika to live."

The chief looked upon him earnestly and asked, "Why? Why are you leaving now?"

The young warrior said carelessly, "Oh, we want to be in a place up high."

The chief, still looking at the young warrior, asked, "How are you going to fish?"

"Oh, we'll come back to do the fishing," he said, still with a careless laugh.

But the chief spoke sadly, "You cannot come. Once you leave the village then you no longer are welcome. If you come back, you will be driven away."

Then the young warrior knew that his ambition had become the cause of exile for his whole family. He knew in his heart that the chief had the true gift of prophecy. And thus they were cast out forever.

The House Entrance
of Kamehameha V

This is the tale just as I have heard it of how King Kamehameha V broke the doorway *kapu* while he was yet a chief, but how he arranged that no blame should attach to him.

Kamehameha had his house, called Malama, built right by the sea, on the foundation from a dwelling which was much older. He ordered the workers to open the front entrance facing the east.

"Oh, *ke ali'i*," the workmen protested, "such a thing is not right. The *kapu* does not permit the entrance to face the rising sun. It cannot be done."

But he refused to listen to them, and at last they obeyed, making his entrance door facing east and the exit door facing west. And when they were finished and it was time to dedicate his home, all the chiefs of the islands and the *kāhuna nui*, who were high priests to the high chiefs, and all the people of Kaunakakai came to the ceremonies.

Everyone could see that the *kapu* had been violated, and the *kāhuna nui* cried out, "You have broken the *kapu*. Surely you have brought your death upon you. Why have you led your people in a crooked path? You are the *ali'i*. It is for you to teach your people the correct way."

The people put their hands to their mouths in horror, but Kamehameha was calm. "No, no," he said. "Does not the law say that the entrance must not face the rising sun? Here is my entrance."

Now, the old foundation was bigger than the new house, thus leaving a platform all around it. And the stone steps on the old foundation went up from the sea, then turned. "*This* is my entrance, facing the sea, up onto the platform and then into the house. My entrance is coming up the steps from the sea and the exit is the same. When you leave the house, you go out on the west end and then you turn and my exit is coming down towards the ocean. Tell me, is this not in keeping with the *kapu*?"

"O prince," said the *kāhuna nui* in great shame and also in great admiration, "it is so, even as you have said."

And thus the people admired Kamehameha V for his great cunning and intelligence in outwitting the *kapu*.

Kaunakakai
and the
Salt Beds of Molokai

When Kapuāiwa, he who would become Kamehameha V, was Minister of Finance for his brother, King Kamehameha IV, he came to a point where he was at his wit's end to raise more money. The sandalwood of Molokai was logged off. Who would want more fish and taro than they could eat? The whalers lived their own lives on their own ships.

It was at this point that a British count visited Kamehameha IV. In conversing with him, Kamehameha IV was very impressed by the count's ready information about finances and sent him to his brother on Molokai with a message: "I am sending this man to you as your guest. He knows a great deal about money, and perhaps he can give you some ideas of how to raise more."

Kapuāiwa greeted him warmly and spent much time with him, discussing with frankness the finances of the kingdom.

Each day, the foreign visitor would sunbathe at Royal Sands, on the sands of the royal beach. One day when he was there, the chiefs of the nearby districts gathered for a *lū'au* that Kapuāiwa was giving in honor of his foreign guest: Chief Ke'eaumoku, Chief Ka'iana, and Chief Kālaimoku. They sat on the beach with the foreign visitor, listening to his stories.

The foreigner had been sunbathing all afternoon, and his skin was as red as the blossom of the hibiscus. Still, he did not leave the beach to escape the rays of the sun. His voice fell silent and he lay as if in a trance, watching the waves ripple over the sandy shore and up on the land.

Then he sprang to his feet and turned excitedly to Kapuāiwa. "O *ali'i nui*," he exclaimed, "may my words seem good to you. Have your men dig *lo'i*, or paddies, where the sea water comes. In this way, the little inlets will hold the water until the sun makes it vanish or until it sinks into the earth. But the salt will remain behind. You can have your own salt beds here, and supply other districts as Ko'olau does. When the cavities are thickly crusted with salt, you can ship it in bags to Honolulu and sell it."

The prince listened carefully and nodded. Next morning, he had his men dig three large *lo'i* where the sea would come. When the tide rose, the salt water flooded into the *lo'i* and immediately drained out through the sand. When the sun was hot, the salt formed a crust at the bottom of the *lo'i.*

Kapuāiwa observed, "There is some dirt in the salt."

The foreign count advised, "Do not use the bottom crust. Let more water come in and let the crusts of salt become thick."

Tide by tide, the plan worked. Each time the water receded, it left a layer of salt particles. After the fifth or sixth tide, the men blocked the entrances to the *lo'i* so they could begin to put the salt into bags. The upper layers were pure and glistening white. When these bags reached Honolulu, they immediately gained for Molokai the reputation of having the best salt in the islands. There was enough to supply the surrounding districts and still sell a great deal.

The stranger stayed for several weeks, an honored guest. One day before he left, he asked Kapuāiwa, "How do you say 'current' in your language?"

"*Kauna*," came the reply. "And sea water is *kahakai*."

"Then let us call this place Kaunakahakai, 'Current of the Sea,' " he suggested.

"So it shall be," said Kapuāiwa, "not least of all in your honor, for *kauna* also means 'nobleman.' "

And thus the district was called Kaunakahakai, its old name. Now it is known as Kaunakakai, "the Town by the Sea."

Malama,
the Summer House Site
of Kamehameha V

When Kamehameha V had a summer house here on Molokai, it was called Malama, "Light." It was made of grass and before it stood a great pole that was highly polished. I myself saw this pole in 1932 and the grass hut as well. It was a puzzle to me why the pole was so polished and why there were hooks in the trees and in the great pole. It was explained to me that his fish, his *poi,* everything, was suspended from hooks so that the rats couldn't get it. The pole was polished so that they could not climb it.

Many *kama'āina*s saw the pole and the grass *hale,* but none of us thought to preserve them or save them.

It was in the area from his house to the coconut grove where Kamehameha V walked daily and in the cool of the evenings. He would not swim here, because silt from the mountains made the ocean muddy; but it was behind his summer house on the beach where he sunbathed. His guests also sunbathed here. The beach was called the Royal Sands because of Kamehameha V and also because Mr. John Owen Dominis, the husband of Queen Lili'uokalani, came here to sunbathe as well. It was once all white sand and secluded.

75

The Poisoned Well

It was in the time of Kamehameha V when the well of sweet water was discovered and also when it was poisoned. Here in this overgrown field, Kamehameha pastured his sheep. They had been given to him as a gift; but he was perplexed, for there was so little water in this part of Molokai that he did not know where to keep them. It was a friend of his, a *kama'āina*, who said, "Let us take them to the high field. Under the big tree is a large boulder. Between its cracks seeps sweet water from a source no one knows about. Come, I will show you."

So the man dug beneath the roots of the tree, and Kamehameha watched it fill up, producing cool, sweet water for his flock.

So matters went for about five years, and the flock prospered. Then a high chief from the east end of Molokai, stung by jealousy of Kamehameha, came to the field and saw the hidden spring. He returned by night and poisoned the water with a weed that the fishermen used to stupefy fish. The sheep drank the water, swelled up, and died. They all died. Inside they were blue from the poison.

Kamehameha V was very angry and made inquiries for many months; but although many people knew who had done it, no one ever told. It was, after all, the business of chiefs only, not of common people.

Tales
of the
North Coast

Hina
and the Aʻe Leaf

This is the tale of Hina and how she found her beloved on the north coast of Molokai.

Hina was a young girl at Waimānalo on the island of Oʻahu when this tale begins. On a clear summer day, her father, Keao, her uncle Iose, and her brother Keola decided to take their canoe toward Molokai. To her joy, she was allowed to accompany them.

As they rounded Makapuʻu Point and could see Molokai in the distance, her heart beat with a strange quickness and a brightness came into her eyes. The men paddled hard and fast across the open sea until they were on the north coast of Molokai. The sun beat down on them, very hot, and soon Hina became drowsy and fell asleep, her left hand trailing in the ocean. In her sleep, her hand touched something in the ocean. Awakening, she clutched it tightly and brought it before her eyes. It was half of a leaf, unknown and strange to her, so she put it in her kīhei to study later.

Then she fell asleep again. In her dream, a young man with a handsome face and body appeared from nowhere and whispered to her, "Take the leaf and go ashore on Molokai. Remain on the island for several days. During that time, you will see the other half of the leaf, and I will claim you for my wife."

Hina awoke with a smile on her lips. Her eyes were shining and her heart beat quickly within her. She felt the warmth of the sun as though it were the warm breath of the young man on her ear, and her heart rejoiced within her. "Quickly," she cried to her father, "pull ashore! Pull ashore!"

He saw at once that something had changed her but replied sensibly, "Wait. I see flat land ahead where we could go ashore. It is too rough and rocky here."

So on they paddled toward the east, but they could not beach the canoe until they came to a short stretch of black sand. They paddled towards it only to find that the current pushed against them, for a stream emptied into the ocean at that point. Hina sat like a statue, her heart already leaping ahead to the shore.

Finally, the men were able to get the canoe close to shore in an eddy. Then they disembarked and each carried a portion of food and clothing to shore. It took many trips, and no one worked harder than Hina.

They found a dry, secluded spot on the sand and made camp for the night. Keola made a fire, and Hina cooked their dinner and put on a large pot for coffee, which, at that time, was not known on Molokai. As they sat around the fire, eating and talking as the coffee brewed, they heard drums beating and the sound of singing and music. Suddenly the drums stopped. They heard voices and saw the light of a torch approaching. Then a voice called out, *"Eō!"*

Keao, being the eldest of the group answered, *"Eō!"*

The visitors came closer and their leader said, "Welcome to Kalaupapa. Please tell us. What is that wonderful smell? When it reached us, we stopped beating the drums and came straight to find you."

Keao and his family hastened to offer them coffee mixed with sugarcane juice and a few drops of milk. It was fragrant and delicious. Each waited a turn to share a cup. When the last visitor had drunk, they all thanked Keao and his family and returned to their village.

Next morning early, no sooner had they completed their morning meal when they heard voices and saw a group of people approaching from the village. Their chief, who had heard the reports of the delicious *kope,* had come himself. Keao expressed his regret that no coffee was brewed. "If you will come in the evening," he promised, "we will make *kope* for you."

Graciously, the chief said, "Your kindness delights me, but this evening you must be my guests at the village. Is it possible that you could bring with you the *kope* of which my people have spoken?"

"We are honored," said Keao. "By all means, we will be there."

Despite his gracious words, Keao was worried. "Hina," he asked, "how much *kope* do we have?"

Hina was also worried. "There is not much, my father," she answered.

Uncle Iose spoke quickly, "Do not be troubled. My nephew sent me a package of Kona *kope* that I have brought with us."

When evening came, Hina, remembering her dream, dressed in her gayest *pā'ū* and bright flowers. She carried the coffee pot, and Uncle Iose brought the Kona coffee. All of them set off for the village.

In the chief's *hale,* they were made welcome and given the places of honor. With many smiles and much laughter, they ate heartily of fish and sweet potatoes. At the end of the meal came a spicy green to eat. "I do not know this plant," observed Keao. "It is delicious and cleansing in the mouth."

The chief told him that it was watercress, which grew well along the streams of the forest. Although no one could have been more gracious and hospitable than the chief, he did not linger over his meal, and his curiosity about the new drink with the delightful fragrance was apparent. Hina brewed the coffee before them all and served him herself, filling his cup to the brim with the rich, dark *kope* and an extra drop of milk to make it sweeter.

With great pleasure, the chief drank his cup and asked for a second cup. Gracefully, Hina poured out a second cup and then poured sips for everyone else around the chief's fire.

Uncle Iose promised to obtain seeds so that they could plant their own *kope* and agreed to show them how to grind the seeds to make the drink. Thus it was that coffee came to Molokai.

All night, they slept in the village, guests of the chief. On the next day, the young people invited Hina and Keola to go with them into the forest. They showed the brother and sister where to gather watercress to take to O'ahu. Hina ate many guavas and felt that Molokai was an island of enchantment. But though she looked at every tree, she saw no leaf like that which had come to her in the ocean. Feeling shy about her dream, even before her brother, she said nothing of it to anyone and did not draw forth her leaf to inquire about it. But her heart was awake in the forest.

For the noon meal, all the young people gathered to share their food in a long and happy celebration of new friendship. After they were finished, they sat in a circle leaning against the tree trunks.

Hina looked up the low cliff rising from the forest floor and suddenly cried out. Halfway down the cliff on a ledge was growing a low tree with large leaves, and one of them—could it be?—was divided in half. Quickly, without explaining her cry, she scrambled up the cliff, reaching from vine to crack to ledge, until she was crouched next to the branch. Instantly she put forth her hand and plucked the divided leaf, then laid it against that which had come to her in the sea. Together they made a complete leaf.

When she came back to the others, they asked her, "What is it? What did you get?" She held up the half-leaf and said carelessly, "Oh, this shape interested me. It is not a bush we have on O'ahu. What is the name of this tree?"

"That leaf comes from the *a'e*, or soapberry tree," answered one of the young men politely. Hina said no more and sat with her eyes cast down to veil their shining.

When it was time to return to their camp, Hina ran all the way. Her father greeted her and said, "Hina, you should sleep this afternoon, for tonight we are bidden to a birthday feast."

Hina felt that she wanted to see no one but be alone with her secret. However, her heart stirred within her strangely, and she thought, "Perhaps it is tonight that he will come."

Obediently she found a quiet place and fell asleep. Several hours later, Keola woke her and told her to get ready to go to the *lū'au*.

Beside her father, she ate the feast as if in a dream and watched the dancing begin. She felt no wish to join the young people in their dancing and romping games. Then, as in her dream, Hina saw a young man coming towards her, extending his hand for her to dance with him. She sprang up, her eyes flashing, her lips curved in a smile of joy, and danced out her secret. Everyone around them smiled and whispered behind their hands.

And thus it was that Hina of O'ahu found her beloved on Molokai and lived her days happily at Kalaupapa, the "Leaf on the Land's Surface."

Wailau,
the Water Leaf

This is the tale of the naming of the village of Wailau, for the mystery of the leaves in the water.

It was many years ago on the beach near one of the valleys on the Koʻolau, or windward, side of Molokai that a man was washed ashore.

Tūtū Naomi and her two sons, Pono and Honukaiakea, gathering pumice stones, ceased their efforts when Pono called out, "Look! A man is floating in the water."

"Quickly!" she instructed them. "Drag him out and bring him to me."

The boys obeyed and rolled him on a large smooth rock so that the salt water would leave his ears and mouth, then brought him to their mother. He was badly bruised and barely alive, but he regained consciousness as the young men carried him to the priest of the village.

"You have found him," the priest told Naomi. "It is for you to say what you will do with him."

Naomi answered, "My sons are grown. They are men. He can share their quarters, and they will help me care for him until he regains his strength."

Pono and Honukaiakea agreed. "Yes, we will take him home with us."

With gratitude, the injured man allowed them to carry him to their home. They stripped off his tattered clothes and bathed his wounds. The *kahuna lapa'au* came to attend him, gave him a large drink of salt water, and ordered him to lie down. In a few moments, he began to vomit blood, and the *kahuna lapa'au* prepared medicine to make the internal bleeding stop. Drop by drop, they laid it on his tongue, commencing again after he vomited it, until at last the vomiting and the bleeding stopped.

"You must watch him with great care," said the *kahuna lapa'au*. "He has lost much strength with his blood. Feed him goat's milk and yams and fish."

All night, Naomi watched carefully over the stranger. She sent her sons deep into the forest at dawn the next day for some special herbs to make him a medicine. It took all day and they returned just as the sun was sinking. She had cooked yams and broiled fish. She had even gone up on the hill to find a goat and patiently milked it, drop by drop obtaining a cup of milk for the stranger.

The next day, the boys woke early to milk the goat, then gathered taro leaves which Naomi cooked. They fished often and saved the best for the stranger.

During the long days of nursing him back to health, he told his new friends that his name was Pekelo and that he lived on Maui at Ke'anae. One day he and his friends went fishing, but their canoe overturned in the rough water. He became separated from them and swam until he was exhausted. The last thing he remembered was clinging to a large log which drifted toward northeast Molokai. Even then, his troubles were not over, for some turtles began swimming with the log, tickling him, nudging him, and bumping him away from the log. He remembered sinking beneath the water, too exhausted to try any more. Then he heard voices and felt himself being rolled back and forth, back and forth. He was in great pain as the water gushed from his mouth and ears, but he could not speak to tell them to stop. He was grateful to them for saving his life.

Before the month was out, he had regained his strength and had begun to work in the taro patches.

When the third month was over, the *kahuna lapaʻau* returned to see him and examined him carefully. Pekelo was in almost perfect health, but on the inner side of his right thigh the *kahuna lapaʻau* found three black circles under the skin.

"These are death circles," he said. "It is fortunate that we know how to cure them."

The next day, he sent Pono to Puʻu o Hōkū for *ʻalaea* and Honukaiakea to the mountains to fetch water from the right bank of a certain waterfall.

Honukaiakea returned with the water, and in the water were leaves from a tree. The plant was foreign to the islands. No one in the village knew the name of the plant or had seen it grow elsewhere.

The *kahuna lapaʻau* examined the leaves and said, "They are good for medicine." Thus, the water and the *ʻalaea* were mixed into a thick paste and applied to the death circles, then exposed to the sun for three hours until it had thoroughly dried. Then Pekelo washed in the ocean. This process was repeated every day for five days, and the death circles disappeared.

Once healed, Pekelo had no wish to return quickly to Maui. "You have made me one of your family. Your home has become my home," he said. "I wish to stay and learn about the cures and medicines you know about in this village."

This he did for one year. Many times, he and the boys went into the mountains above the waterfall, looking for the tree whose leaves had appeared in the water. They saw nothing and it remained a great mystery.

After a year, Pekelo told Naomi and her sons, "I have been here for a year. I must go home now or my family will begin the mourning ceremonies for someone lost at sea. I will always remember you as my second family. Please come at any time to my home in Ke'anae on Maui and there you will become as my family."

On the day of his departure, the people of the village gave a huge *lū'au* to celebrate his return to life and his return to his family. They presented him with a canoe in which to make his return voyage. Pekelo, after the *lū'au*, bade farewell to the goats on the hill whose milk had nourished him when he was dangerously ill. Then he climbed to the right bank of the waterfall and filled a calabash with the water, being sure to also take some of the mysterious leaves.

He kissed everyone with tears running down his cheeks. He clung to Naomi and her sons. "*Aloha* to you all, my kind friends. I shall always remember you. And what shall I tell my people is the name of this valley?"

The *kahuna nui* said, "This valley has no name."

Pekelo took the calabash from his canoe and poured the water on the land where the stream entered the ocean. "Then I name this valley Wailau, 'Water Leaf,' " he said. And thus he departed.

The mystery of the plant has never been solved. The people called it *lau ola*, "leaf of life," and the valley still bears the name, Wailau, that Pekelo gave it so long ago.

Pio,
the Bird Bride
of Hālawa

This is the tale of Manukula and the birds of Hālawa.

It was many years ago when Chief Kapioho ordered Manukula to live on Moku Hoʻoniki, the little island near Kepuhi on the east end of Molokai. Only birds lived on this little island, the lovely birds of Molokai who were protected and cherished for their beauty. It was because Manu loved birds that he was sent there to live. Indeed, his name means "bird of the uplands."

He was given a canoe and spears and was allowed to kill any bird of prey that would have destroyed the island birds. He came to Molokai to fetch fresh water for these birds to bathe in, and soon, many new birds came to the island to live. Soon they would come when Manu whistled or called the names he had given them. His happiness would have been complete but for one thing. He was very lonely.

At last, he paddled across to Molokai and told Chief Kapioho of his loneliness. "May I not marry so that I may have a wife for company?" he asked. The chief spoke to the *kahuna*, but the *kahuna* told the chief: "Manu may not marry any woman known to him. He must wait. In a dream he will learn where he must go to find his wife."

Surprised and puzzled, Manu returned to his island. It was not many nights later when a dream came to him. In the dream, he was told to return to Molokai and walk along the shore toward the north until he came to a cleft in the land. "Walk into that valley towards the upland," said the voice in his dream. "Then you will be instructed what you must do."

The voice from the dream still seemed fresh in his ears when he awoke the next morning. Without hesitation, he took his canoe and paddled across to Molokai. On the beach, he started walking north along the coastline until he came to a hill, Kapu'upo'i. By then he was tired, so he sat and rested. As his eye followed the shape of the hill, he noticed a cleft in the land and promptly scrambled to his feet. In the narrow ravine was a faint trail heading upland. This was Hālawa Gulch and he was walking up to the falls of Hālawa Valley.

It was a difficult climb. Soon he became faint from hunger, as he had not paused to eat before leaving his island. "*Auwē*," he reproached himself, "in such haste I came that I forgot to bring food. What can I do?"

Just then he noticed a guava bush heavily laden with ripe fruit. In the bush perched a little bird, chirping prettily and pecking on a guava. Suddenly, he could understand her song. She was saying, "Come, Manukula. You are in your home. Come and eat. There is plenty of food. The mountain-apples are ripe too. Come, let us eat together."

Manu was astonished at the bird's words, but he took some guavas and ate heartily as he continued his climb up the trail. His heart beat fast. Strange feelings stirred within him. He knew from his dream that he would find a bride this day.

Just as he glimpsed the waterfall, the little bird fluttered down to his shoulder, and her voice sounded softly in his ear, "From here on you must change to a bird or you can go no further."

In a day of astonishments, this instruction was the most astonishing. "I have never changed to a bird before," said Manu. "Is it possible that I can do so?"

Obediently, he climbed a large rock and prepared to leap. "I am Manukula!" he shouted. Then he leaped and immediately his arms became wings, and he soared upward to the trees. He perched on a branch of a tall tree and said, "I am ready to receive more instructions."

His little bird flew by and chirped softly, "Follow me." Together they flew to the top of Hīpuapua Falls. There in the top pool was a young girl catching 'ōpae (shrimp). On a stone nearby was a big red bird watching the young girl. Manu knew at once that he was in the presence of his bride, but his confusion did not disappear. "Is my chosen wife the bird or the girl?" he asked. "I do not wish to remain a bird."

He swooped into flight once more, circling the bird and the girl. As he came close to the red bird, his little friend chirped, "Do not touch the red bird or you will be obliged to marry her, and she is already married to the *mo'o* of the next falls. Quickly fly to the young girl and touch her ears."

Manu obeyed quickly. The girl laughed and reached up her hand. Manu allowed her to catch him, singing and chirping coaxingly. She was delighted with him, left her shrimp, and quickly returned to the village with Manu on her shoulder. She went to seek the *kahuna* and said, "O *kahuna*, behold this bird which flew near the falls and came to my hand. He will not now leave my shoulder. What can this mean?"

The *kahuna* answered at once, "It is a sign that he wishes to marry you. Do you wish to be his wife?"

Without hesitation, she said, "Yes, oh yes, but can you change him into a man?"

No sooner had she expressed her desire than Manu changed back into his human form. She looked into his eyes and smiled with pleasure, then lowered her eyes in confusion because he was so handsome.

Manu took her hand. "What is your name?"

Her eyes darting about him like birds, she said softly, "Pio is my name."

"What a strange name it is," said Manu.

"I was named Pio because when my mother gave birth to me, she kept hearing the birds of the forest chirping *pio, pio.*"

"Your name is wonderful to me," said Manu. "My name is Manukula and we shall call *pio, pio,* all the time."

The *kahuna* told Pio, "When you are pregnant, you must come back to Hālawa to give birth to the child. Manu must come, too, to plant taro in the valley. Thus, it is certain that he will remain human and will always have a place for his family here in Hālawa."

They listened to him with shining eyes and agreed to do as he said. Then they left the village and began descending to Kapuʻupoʻi, the hill at the beginning of the cleft in the land where the ocean curves along the shoreline of Hālawa Valley.

It is said they went back to Moku Hoʻoniki and lived happily. Manukula died after many years, for he was too human to survive forever on a barren island without trees, a cool breeze, and the mist of waterfalls. Whenever the people hear *pio, pio,* the call of the birds, they remember Manukula and his lovely bride, Pio. In Hālawa, they say, "Oh, Pio will have another child." Strange to say, every child she had after Manu died was a bird.

Thus, when you are in Hālawa Valley and you hear the *pio, pio* of the birds, you can be sure it is a child of Pio's.

I myself have heard them.

The Valley
of Pelekunu

Three valleys run inland on the northeast coast of Molokai—Pelekunu, Wailau, and Hālawa.

The valley of Pelekunu is so long and narrow that the sun does not shine into it for much of the day, and people seeking a new home seldom stay in it. In 1836, so it is said, the valley had just 218 people; in 1900, 302—nearly all of them kin to one another. And now I do not know, because so much is different.

Pelekunu's people, in the days I remember, would rise early—perhaps at five-thirty every morning—to make use of the sun for their chores. All the women and girls would gather up the laundry and go down to the stream. They would wash the clothes in the running water, then spread them out on the grass to dry with stones on them so the wind wouldn't blow them away.

The men wore pants and sometimes undershirts. The women wore "taro-patch pants," the trousers their husbands had worn through at

95

the knee which the women cut shorter and wore with a rope tied around the waist or with suspenders. On the top they would wear *pale 'ili*, or short-sleeved clinging cotton shirts, also borrowed from their husbands. Children just wore short pants and *pale 'ili* too.

While the women were doing the laundry, the men and boys would gather fuel and light fires on their outdoor stoves to boil water for their *nehe*, or tea, and to cook their taro. They always drank tea in the morning to cleanse the body internally.

At seven o'clock, everyone would eat breakfast: *nehe*, slices of taro, lots of guavas and mountain-apples or whatever fruits were in season.

After breakfast, some of the men would go fishing in the ocean while the rest went into the taro patch to work. The women also would divide, some fishing in the stream for *'o'opu*, which is also known as catfish, and *hīhīwai*, or shellfish, and the rest gathering taro leaves and snails from the taro patch.

At about nine o'clock, the women would return and begin to prepare the food they had gathered. They would cook the taro leaves and snails, mix the *poi*, broil the fish they had caught in the stream, and boil the *hīhīwai*. Usually, the food was ready before the fishermen had come back from the ocean with their catch. When they came, everyone would eat *poi* or sweet potatoes, dried fish, lots of the fresh fish raw, and any fruit in season—mountain-apple or guava or any fruit they had found.

The fishermen might bring in *limu*, *pūpū*, which is a shellfish, many other kinds of fish, and turtle—all except the white turtle. The white turtle is the *'aumakua*, or family god, of the Pelekunu people, so it is forbidden to catch and to eat this variety. But with all other kinds of turtle they took at sea, they would cut the meat into long thin strips, salt it, and set it out to dry in the sun for those days when they were not lucky in their fishing.

Near the cove of Pelekunu is a large cave called Keanapuhi, the Cave of the Eel. The fishermen would often go there to catch the large moray eel. When it is skinned and cut into fillets and broiled over charcoal, it tastes like chicken fricassee.

In the narrow valley of Pelekunu, food was plentiful from the land and from the sea; and each member of the family had a task in gathering or catching food, in preparing it to be cooked or eaten raw.

After this second meal, only a few hours remained before the shadows met and darkened the valley. It was the time for the children to play or go swimming. The women would rest or do chores. Often the menfolk went to the uplands to lay traps for wild pigs that might come down from the mountain to eat guava around the taro patch. They would scatter taro peelings under the guava trees as bait for the trap. And if they caught a pig, they roasted it and everyone feasted; but since they hadn't acquired a real taste for pork, they didn't care much whether they were successful in trapping a pig or not.

At five o'clock, it would be dusk. Everybody would go down to the sea to bathe, the children first, then the young people, and last the mothers and the fathers.

At six o'clock, they would eat their last meal of the day: *poi*, sweet potato, raw fish with cooked *limu*, vegetables such as taro leaf, or spinach, and *ung choi*, a swamp cabbage that grew wild in the taro patches.

After that, there would be a devotional service in their living quarters. The father would read to them from the Hawaiian Bible. The neighbors who did not own a Bible would join with a family that did. They would sing together and pray. They were very religious. Their religion was Kalawina, or Calvinism. After the coming of the missionaries, the people would travel for miles to go to the church in Kalua'aha in the eastern part of Molokai and would climb over the ridge twice every year to attend the Sunday school *hō'ike* at Wailau in the next valley.

Those were the days of happiness and peace in the valley of Pelekunu. The earth was good to them and people worked together, sharing and caring for one another.

97

The Valley
of Wailau

And now I will relate the way things came to pass in Wailau Valley.

People in Wailau Valley lived in a fashion much like that of the people of Pelekunu. However, they were more "advanced" than in Pelekunu. One of the largest families in the valley owned a store and brought in hardware and dry goods by sampan (small boat) to sell to the people of the three valleys. In one wing of the store was a school. The family lived above on the second floor with their many children.

Wailau also had a man trained to be a medicinal herb doctor, a *kahuna lapa'au*. This is a very serious occupation. He spent seven years being trained by the old herb doctor and then was blessed by the priest of the valley as a full-fledged doctor.

He would spend most of his time cultivating herbs that were difficult to find and had a regular herb garden. He grew yams in the garden, but they were special—only for medicinal purposes.

Anyone caught stealing his yams was punished. The thief had to accompany the *kahuna lapa'au* when he went in search of herbs on the other side of the island, which he did twice a year. The thief had to pack their food and sleeping gear, see to the needs of the *kahuna lapaʻau*, prepare all the meals, and carry back the heavy load of herbs when they returned to Wailau.

Like Pelekunu, the people of Wailau lived as one harmonious family, sharing food and possessions, caring for each other. Taro grew wild in the valley with many other plants that they could eat and fish that they could catch.

Their *ʻaumakua*, family guardian, was the *manini*, a fish that is sort of grayish green with black and white stripes. At the mouth of the stream that empties into the bay at Wailau is a *koʻa*, or shrine, to the *manini*. It is a big stone shaped exactly like a *manini*. And strange though it may seem, the stone is grayish and the moss grows on the stone in stripes that make black bars. The top of the stone was shaped perfectly like the back of the *manini*. Every day the people would go down to the mouth of the stream and give the *manini koʻa* the liver of the other fishes. That's why the *manini heiau* was called Manini-ai-ake, "Manini-devours-liver."

Nobody caught or ate the *manini* that lived in this stream. Indeed, it was seldom that they ate *manini* caught elsewhere either, because it was their *ʻaumakua*.

They also were Kalawina in their religion, and twice a year they would have a Sunday school rally, or *hōʻike*. Then the people from Pelekunu Valley would climb over the ridge to join them, and the members of the Kalawina group in Kalaupapa would canoe around the bend and join them. The *hōʻike* would end with a feast of *kālua* pig and all the other delicacies that they could acquire from the valley. For the *hōʻike*, the women would dress up as they did on Sundays, in dresses or *muʻumuʻus*.

The Reverend Dennis Kamakahi was so inspired by the valley when he went there to visit that he composed the popular song, "Hīhī-wai," which says, "Return to the valley, the beautiful peaceful valley."

Beauty, peace . . . that is the valley of Wailau.

The Valley
of Hālawa

Now I will begin the story of Hālawa Valley.

This is the largest and the most beautiful of all the three valleys. In it is a large river fed by two waterfalls. These two waterfalls, Moaʻula and Hīpuapua, meet and their river flows down into the ocean in the center of this valley.

The river has both fish and crab in it. On both sides of this big river are taro patches that are watered by little streams. Taro grows very well in the valley and supplies the rest of the island with *poi*.

The school there was taught by a young Hawaiian named David Kalaʻau. Not only did he teach the students their ABC's, but he taught them music as well. The young voices of the students would blend beautifully because of the way he trained them. In the evening, he trained their parents. Whenever they went off the island for music festivals, they would usually rank first in their category. Their voices were full and rich; and they pronounced the Hawaiian words with clarity and precision, because Mr. Kalaʻau demanded it.

The Hālawa School also held the record for its pupils' having no cavities for all the years Mr. Kala'au taught in the valley. It was not particularly because of him that there were no cavities but because there were no fast foods or sweets to eat.

Mr. Kala'au was an intelligent, happy, kind man and was a teacher, preacher, song leader, counselor, advisor, and beloved friend to the people of Hālawa.

The Lost Tunnel
of Pelekunu

This tale was told to me by Akoni Keaka, who heard it from his mother when he was young. She lived in Pelekunu with her family and Akoni, her lover, lived in Kamalō. When the weather was bad, he used to walk the Kamalō Trail to Pelekunu to court her. However, when the weather was fair, he would go over to Pelekunu from Hālawa by canoe.

On one trip, he paddled to Pelekunu to visit her but could not return home. The ocean was too rough to go by canoe and the trail had been washed out by the rain. But he had to go home, for he had promised to help his father with the fishpond. He was so determined to get back to Kamalō that he made a desperate decision. Many tales were told of a tunnel between Pelekunu and Kamalō. People were afraid of it and its mystery, and its exact location had been lost.

"I will walk the tunnel trail," he announced.

His beloved pleaded with him not to go, but his resolution did not waver. Thus, she did her part by going to every family to ask if anyone knew where the tunnel entrance was. Kaleihoolau, a *kama'āina*, at last said, "Yes, I know where it is, but I do not know whether it is still in use. If you are determined, I will show you where it is."

Akoni, followed by his love, went to the northeastern part of the valley, and there on the side of the cliff they saw a cave. "That is the entrance to the tunnel," Kaleihoolau told them.

Akoni kissed his love *aloha* and entered the cave.

For the first 250 feet, light gleamed in from the entrance, dimmer, dimmer, and then sheer darkness. He lit his torch and slowly groped his way through the tunnel. He walked for hours.

He began to feel dizzy and nauseated, so he sat down to rest. As he rested, he realized that he was having difficulty in breathing. He knew that he had to get air, so he lurched to his feet and staggered on, on and on, how long he could not tell. He knew that the torch was burning up the oxygen in the tunnel, but the thought of blowing it out and going forward in the dark was a nightmare to him.

Finally, he saw a glimmer of light ahead. Quickly he blew out his torch and kept moving toward the light. He stumbled often and fell several times, but he moved on. The light grew brighter, and the fresh air blowing into the cave gave him the vigor to move faster. When he came to the exit, he stumbled through and leaned, panting, against the rocks, grateful to be alive and able to think at last about what it might mean that the tunnel was there and could still be used.

Turning again to the cave, he cried, *"Māhalo,"* thanking whatever spirit had guided him through the tunnel.

As he moved into the warm sunlight, he realized that he was on the west end of his own property just south of Ioli Gulch. His parents were astonished to see him.

His father said, "I have been watching the ocean to see you paddling your canoe, but I had given up hope that you could come today. How is it that you come now and from this direction?"

With great excitement Akoni cried, "There is a tunnel to Pelekunu, and it comes out on our property. Now I can go to Pelekunu through the tunnel whenever I wish."

The next day he took his father to see the entrance, then he told his story many times to the people of Kamalō. He did not forget to tell them of the place of dizziness and suffocation in the middle of the mountain, so no one who was ill or had trouble breathing was allowed to go, and anyone using the tunnel always told Akoni and his family when they were going.

And thus, the lost tunnel became known again. But after Akoni and his love were married, he had no need to go through the mountain to see her.

Tales of
My Own
Molokai

Ransom for the Giant Squid

Where the road curves by Kūpeke on Molokai, going eastward on the island, a great stone marked with white paint stands beside the fishpond. Beneath it, arching black into the water, is a hole like a small cave. Here lives the giant squid,* and he holds travelers on the road to ransom when they come past bearing cooked pork. Ah, how that squid loves pork!

Now it is the custom at parties to give guests a *pū'olo*, or bundle, of food to take home. It could be fish, it could be *poi*, or it could be *kūlolo*, pudding of grated taro and coconut. But usually it is pork—*kālua* pig roasted in a pit or *laulau* pig, which has been steamed in ti leaves.

Ah, it is good! And it is the pork, especially the pork, that the giant squid desires. If you are driving—fast or slow—your car will stop at

---

*In modern Hawai'i, the octopus *(he'e)* is familiarly called "squid," as in "squid *lū'au*."

this curve. You will notice an object in the road, eight or nine feet tall. It will be the giant squid, blocking the road. If you turn to drive to the left, it will move to the left. If you turn to the right, it will move to the right. And so you must throw it your bundle. When you do, the giant squid will slide off the road and let you pass. If you look back, you will see it pick up the bundle and disappear under the great rock.

Tales of this squid go back past my grandmother's grandmother's day, and further—back into the 1600s. So the local folks know that if they are traveling past Kūpeke to Kaunakakai—and there is only this one road—they must not refuse to give up their pork. So they are wise. They accept anything but pork from their hostess.

I myself have seen this squid.

Once it happened that I was camping with a friend from Kaunaka-kai at a health center on the eastern road, and we were invited to a party. At its end, our hostess asked me to take home some food. I refused, but my friend seemed to have forgotten about the legend—or perhaps she did not know it, for she is not from Molokai.

"Why, thank you," said Jean to our hostess. "I think Mike would enjoy some pork."

Our hostess gave her a *pu'olo* of pork wrapped up very nicely with sweet potatoes, and we started off in Jean's car.

I said nothing about the squid as we drove; but suddenly, just at the curve, the car skidded and stopped.

"My gosh!" exclaimed Jean. "What's the matter?" She stared ahead into the darkness. "Is that a telephone pole in the middle of the road?" Then she laughed at herself and said, "I must be too far on the left."

She tried to pass on the right, but the object moved to the right. She looked out of the window and saw that she was in the middle of the road. Then she saw that the telephone pole was at the side of the road where it belonged but that the object was still blocking her way.

"It's the squid!" she exclaimed. "We're at Squid Rock."

She climbed out of the car and said, "I'm taking this *pu'olo* home for my husband, but I will share it with you." She took out some

pork, wrapped it in foil, and tossed it to the squid. She began praying as she got back into the car, for she is Catholic.

She put the car in gear and started forward. But as she approached the squid, it did not move. Instead, with one of its great tentacles, it seized the car's bumper and began yanking on it.

"Stop!" she cried. "Wait. I'll give you the rest."

So she threw the whole bundle out of the window. The tentacle released the car, and the giant squid slid off the road. Jean drove very fast all the way home.

Some time later, Jean and I were together with our new doctor, Dr. Wood and his wife. They both like to hear stories about Molokai, so I told Jean to tell them about the giant squid. She didn't want to. "They have to travel by that highway, and it will only make them nervous," she protested.

But they were both interested, so at last she told them of our experience. Mrs. Wood would not believe it. "No, no," she insisted. "I can't believe it. Not in this day."

But Dr. Wood was different. He looked at us and said, "If you had told me this story, Harriet, I would wonder about it, because you are local. But Jean is not. And I have heard before of the giant squid. Yes, I believe it."

The Ghost Tree
of 'Ōhi'a

The tale of Keala's daughter is a tale of old times, but this is a tale of 'Ōhi'a Gulch that was told to me by a friend named Mele.

On certain nights in the year she saw a person dressed in a long white robe, walking with a limp on the trail leading up into the ravine called 'Ōhi'a'ai. It seemed to her to be a spirit, but she watched for it and waited for it.

One night she followed this being, but it disappeared when it came to a small stream. Returning home, she waited for dawn, then went to the stream. There she saw small footprints that had sunk deep into the soft earth with a fresh mountain-apple seed lying beside them. She left everything as it was and returned home.

But the next day she told her neighbor, Bill Meyer, what she had seen. Bill did not believe it was a ghost, but he was as curious as Mele.

"Could it be So-and-So? Or So-and-So?" he asked, naming neighbors that he thought might be the mysterious person. He asked Mele many questions about when it appeared and how it walked. His conclusion was: "It must be a woman because the footprints are small. Also, she must be heavyset because the prints are deep in the ground. And because she limps, it must be Maggie. But where did she disappear to? There is no other trail nearby where she can get home without anyone seeing her."

Mele agreed with Bill that the ghost must be Maggie, but the mystery remained.

It was not until the following summer that the ghost reappeared. Bill was talking story with Mele's husband after dark one night. The young moon had risen, giving a little light. Mele, who had gone outside for a few minutes, suddenly cried, "Bill, come quickly."

In the pale moonlight they saw the ghostlike figure going up the trail. They both followed slowly, some distance behind. Yes, it seemed to be Maggie. But when the figure came to the stream they saw her no more. They ran to the spot but found no one. So they returned home.

The next day they went back to the spot and were surprised to see a new mountain-apple tree about five feet tall which had never been there before. Then Mele remembered the first *'ōhi'a 'ai* seed.

"Is it not a tree grown from that seed?" she demanded. "It stands at exactly at the spot where I saw the seed. And is the figure then not the Ghost of 'Ōhi'a'ai, since it can make this tree grow in a single year?"

They returned home, feeling that they had found the answer, even though Bill did not believe in ghosts.

The following summer, Mele went to the stream to gather some red *'ōhi'a 'ai*. Much to her surprise, she found the ghost's tree loaded with fruits, big and shiny but very pale. She plucked one and opened it. To her astonishment it was white, instead of red like the rest of the trees in the surrounding ravine.

This mountain-apple tree is now very tall. I myself have talked to Mele and she often picks its fruit. Now it is both red and white, very juicy. And it is still mysterious.

Pu'uhonua,
the Place of Refuge

It is not far from Kamakou where the ruined *pu'uhonua*, or place of refuge, of Molokai lies within stone walls. In ancient times, those who had angered the chief or the *kāhuna* and were in danger of death could go and stay—sometimes five years, sometimes seven years— within the enclosure. But at the end of that time, they were pardoned.

I myself have seen this place, and I know of a Chinese man who was accused of smuggling opium from China to Honolulu. The F.B.I. were very close to capturing him when he heard of his danger and fled to Molokai. First, he visited his wife and many children on the east end, and then he went to the *pu'uhonua*. His wife knew nothing of this place, but he had heard about it from the *kama'āina*s.

After he had been there for almost seven years, the F.B.I. heard where he was staying and came up. They did not enter the *pu'uho-nua*, for they respected the sacred places of Hawai'i. But they waited. Then when he emerged, they captured him.

It was a very famous case, for his defense was not about the opium at all but about the seven years he had spent in the *pu'uhonua*. His lawyer was old man Trask, who knew all the old ways. It is said that he got the book of laws and showed the court exactly where it says that if you stay in a *pu'uhonua* for more than five years, you are no longer guilty of a crime.

The lawyer for the F.B.I. laughed. "That is the old law. That law has no power."

"But it has not been amended or changed or cancelled out," said old man Trask.

And the judge ruled that the law was still in force. But after that, the legislature amended the laws, and now the *pu'uhonua* is in ruins.

The Coconut Grove
of the Five Springs

I will tell you of the coconut grove of the five springs.

The first spring is called the farmers' spring. In ancient times the *kama'āina*s would bathe after working in the village or on the farms.

The second spring was the community spring. After washing in the farmers' spring, the men would join the fishermen and women and children in the biggest spring.

Next to the big spring is the drinking-water spring, which no one ever bathed in because it provided drinking water for the whole community. This spring, though it is covered by salt water, still bubbles up fresh and sweet.

On the shore of the fourth spring the fishermen would put all of the fish, the shellfish, and the seaweed they brought to the shore. The women would then go to this spring to clean and scale the fish, laying them on the coral reef to dry, then bringing them home when they were ready. I myself call this pool the kitchen-sink spring.

The fifth spring was called the menstrual spring. During their time

of menstruation each month, it was *kapu* for the women to bathe in the community spring, and this spring was reserved for them.

When I was a child, when we first moved over to the homestead, the school used to be right across from the menstrual spring. We walked past it on our way to school each day. And for three days out of every month, that water would be red, red, red.

I myself have seen it.

The Night Marchers
of Molokai

Now I will tell you about the night marchers. I myself have seen them on Molokai.

It is in the season called October and November that they come. They come walking, walking, and chanting as they walk.

When I was a child, one of my friends was a teacher at the school. On a certain evening, she said, "I need to go to my classroom to work tonight, but I do not want to go by myself."

"I will come with you gladly," I said.

Together we walked to the school. As she busied herself at her desk, the sound of chanting came to us. "What is that, Harriet?" she asked.

I knew at once what it was although I had never heard it before, but I said to her only, "It's just someone chanting."

"No," she said, rubbing her arms. "I am getting gooseflesh. Who is it really?"

"I think it is the night marchers going fishing," I said. "Let us go outside and watch."

At first she did not wish to, but then she became curious. We sat on the floor by the classroom door so that they could not see us and looked through the doorway. The chanting came closer and closer. The first man was tall and strong, of the chief's class. All of them carried torches but the light did not shine on their faces, only on their bodies and legs.

"I did not believe in night marchers," said my friend. "When my husband, who was born here, would speak of them I would only laugh, for I am from Italy. Now I see that it is so. Where are they going?"

"They will go down to the beach, following a pathway in a straight line," I said. "Kapuni built his house with the kitchen right across their path, even though he knew that they will not turn to the right or to the left."

And so it was. Even as we watched, they continued down the hill to the house and then disappeared inside.

Years afterwards, my Aunt Hattie, for whom I was named, bought Kapuni's home and we would visit her on weekends. One day I said, "Auntie Hattie, I wish to come here in October and sleep."

"Why?" she asked. "Is it to celebrate your birthday?"

"Of course," I said, "but it is also to see the night marchers."

"Indeed yes," she said and laughed. "They will come through the house. You will not even need to go outside."

And so it was arranged. My father, my mother, and my brothers and sister came to stay with Auntie Hattie.

On the night of the march, we sat in her house. On her countertop was a large and unusual calabash in which she kept her eggs. As we talked, I noticed that the calabash was rocking back and forth.

"What is it?" I asked her.

"It is the night marchers," she answered. "They approach."

119

I rose and approached the calabash. "The eggs are clicking together. The calabash is rocking hard. Surely the eggs will be broken?"

"Do not worry," she said. "In five years, never has one egg cracked."

Then I looked out of the window and saw the line of torches approaching in a straight line, first the chief, then the *kahuna*, then the lesser chief, and then the fishermen carrying their nets. I heard their chanting.

My brother was scornful of them. "I am going to sleep here," he said, pointing to a place on the floor.

"No, no," said my aunt. "That is where they will walk."

"I want to see if they will walk on me," he said.

"Yes, they will," she insisted. "Do not be foolish."

"Ah, I don't believe it," he said and lay down on the floor. Just as my aunt saw the marchers coming through the door, she snatched my brother away. As they went by, he tried to catch one of the legs of a fisherman, but the night marcher lifted his leg higher and kept marching.

And that is what happened in 1958.

The Old Warrior
of Hanakeakua

Ⅰt was Kailau Kaleikua who told me the tale of the ancient warrior of Hanakeakua, and it was Kailau Kaleikua who showed me the old warrior, even though my father could see nothing. And this is how it happened.

As a young man, Kailau worked for Molokai Ranch. As his work brought him to the Kīpū area one evening, he saw an elderly Hawaiian sitting on the side of a little hill, puffing on *kapaka*, a cigarette made from a roll of tobacco leaves. As he drew on his cigarette, the light from its glowing end illuminated his face and body. His face was wrinkled and he was nearly bald, but his body was strong and beautiful, gleaming through a brown *malo* the color of his skin.

Many nights Kailau saw this person and gazed upon him with admiration and respect, but he never spoke to him. After many months, he summoned up his courage and approached the old man. To his surprise, as he neared the old man's seat, the man stood and greeted him. His voice was kind, but Kailau's courage deserted him and his voice shook as he responded.

121

The man invited him to sit by his side and offered Kailau some tobacco leaves so he could roll his own cigarette. Kailau refused, saying he did not smoke. The man spoke in Hawaiian with a low voice, but the pronunciation was very distinct.

Kailau remarked, "You must be a scholar of the chief's court."

The man explained, "No. I am a warrior and I fight for the chief. I train every day. I *haki* (break or snap) and I excel in using the weapons of war."

Kailau's fear was gone and he said, "You must be strong. You have a beautiful body."

The old warrior laughed, "You don't have to be strong to be a good warrior. You must use your brains as well as muscles. And you have to be skilled in the use of the implements of war."

Kailau returned the next night and gave the warrior an 'alā, or stone disk, inscribed with symbols of good fortune. The warrior gladly accepted it and was grateful. He later made it into a neckpiece which he always wore around his neck.

For many months, Kailau came to talk with the old man whenever he was on that end of the island. One evening when Kailau came after an absence of several weeks, the old warrior was not there. Kailau went to the village of Hanakeakua to inquire about him. There the chief told him that the old warrior had died in a battle two weeks earlier.

The next day when the sun rose, Kailau made his way to the battlefield and began to search among the bones for the old warrior. He walked among the bones, stooping to inspect every skull that he came across. On the third day of his search, he found the 'alā he had given the old man and recognized the nearby skeleton as that of the warrior. Respectfully, he gathered all the bones and took them to the old warrior's favorite hillside, and buried them there.

Many *kama'āina*s say that they have seen the old warrior, sitting on his hillside and smoking in the evening. And I myself have seen him.

The Old Warrior

It came about in this way. Often at night, my mother and I would go riding with my father in our flatbed Chevrolet truck, accompanying him but saying nothing to disturb him as he breathed the night air and meditated. One night, Kailau Kaleikua wished to accompany us.

We went along in silence, all four of us, Kailau next to my father and I next to my mother. Suddenly, Kailau said to my mother and me quietly in Hawaiian, "Look to your right, on the hill."

I looked and said, "I see a man smoking."

"Yes," he said, "that's the old warrior."

My mother also saw him, but my father asked, "Where is he?"

We pointed to the spot and his face turned toward the glowing light of the old man's cigarette, but he saw nothing. I asked Kailau, "How is it that Papa cannot see?"

"Not everyone can see these things," he responded. "Your mother can see because she is Hawaiian, but your father is a true Christian. He cannot gaze on the past and the present for it has no importance to Christianity."

I was bursting with questions, but he shook his head at me softly and I said no more.

Kailau Kaleikua has been dead for many years now; but even today, people see the old warrior sitting on the hill, the glow of his *kapaka* lighting up his ancient face and his strong, beautiful body.

The Mū

Few, indeed, are the people who have seen the Mū, a rough, short, and stumpy people who live in caves on the side of a cliff facing the ocean on the island of Molokai. Sometimes they do evil, sometimes good; but they are a people from before the ancient times, and what is good or evil to them?

I myself have seen them.

It came about in this way. When I was a girl in school in 1928, only thirteen years old, one of my classmates named Ella was kidnaped by an old man, fifty years old. He had asked her to marry him and kidnaped her when she refused.

Because he knew that her family would bring the police and begin searching at once, he took her to a cave in the cliffs that already had old clothes and bits of canvas in it. He caught fish for her to eat and fetched water from three springs arranged in a triangle, going out only by night and always keeping her under watch or tied up so that she could not call or escape.

The children also were enlisted in the search, each of us with a long stick to poke into bushes and under rocks, for we did not know if she was still alive. Ten paces apart we were, and we went over the whole island.

When we came to the place where the trail goes to the cliff, the sheriff said, "Do not go on the trail. The police will go to the beach below and search. It is too dangerous." He did not wish any of the children to be injured.

But I was curious, so I asked, "May I go with the policemen?" And he gave me permission—"if they are willing that you should go."

Among the four policemen that he assigned to go down the trail was Charlie, an old man, wise and very friendly to my family. He gave me permission to accompany him, and we started down the trail. It became slippery, the smooth dirt slanting toward the ocean far below. We had to cling to vines and walk on stones. In some places there was nothing to cling to, so I dug my fingers into the earth until my nails broke and my fingers bled.

But although the trail was very narrow and dangerous, it led us to the caves.

"You are small," said Charlie. "Crouch down and go through that *puka* and tell us what you see."

He gave me his flashlight, and I crawled through the entrance.

"What do you see in there?" he called.

"Somebody is living here," I called back. "There are old clothes and a blanket and some fish bones and *'opihi* shells."

"Is it Ella?" he asked.

"No," I answered. "The smell is terrible and the air is foul. It would not be possible for anyone to stay in here longer than a few minutes, and Ella would become ill. I am getting a terrible pain in my head already."

"Come out and breathe the fresh air from the ocean," he said.

As I climbed back through the *puka,* my eye fell upon a sash. I knew at once it was Ella's.

"Quickly," I cried. "I know she is here. We have dresses alike—hers red and white and mine green and white. Here is the sash from her dress."

Immediately the three slender policemen returned with me to the cave. We found a gallon bottle of drinking water but no sign of Ella.

"Please give me your flashlight," I said to one of the policemen. "There is a passage going back into the darkness and perhaps she is there."

"I will come with you," he said.

Together we went back into the darkness. Suddenly we stopped. Against the wall of the cave stood five or six people. They did not move or speak, but their eyes glinted in the light as they watched us. They had only a cloth wrapped around them. Their hair was long and thick, but they had no beards or mustaches on their wrinkled brown faces. The muscles on their legs seemed to leap out in the light from the flashlight.

We backed quickly away into the chamber and listened for a moment. No sound came to us. "Say nothing," said the policeman. "She is not there. They are the last tribe of the Mū people, here before the Hawaiians came."

I had never heard of the Mū. Later I heard an old chant by the *kama'āina*s who lived near the cliff, and the Mū appear in that chant. Sam Burrows, who is now dead, once said he saw very wide, very flat footprints in the sand of the beach—Mū going to fish.

And we did not find Ella, though we were close. Three months later, the sheriff was hunting in the gullies near the cliff with Ella's dog, and the dog found her. She was almost dead. They took her to Maui where she was put in a special hospital until she recovered. The old man was still working in the pineapple fields, so they arrested him and put him in jail on Maui.

After Ella was well again, they brought her back to Molokai, but she refused to go to school. She was ashamed. She cried and cried. Finally her parents took her and moved away. I do not know what became of her.

The Menehune

The Mū are not the only ancient people from before the time the Hawaiians came. No, even before the Mū were the Menehune, and I have seen them both on Hawai'i and on Kaua'i. It happened this way in the year that I went to Kaua'i, in 1936 or 1938.

On Kaua'i are caves, and inside one cave is a large ledge. That is where they live, eating only guava and fish or perhaps taro. One day when I was there with friends, two men said, "The Menehune are on the beach fishing. Come quietly. Make no noise." So cautiously I approached the cliff overlooking the beach and saw their backs and heads as they fished.

We were there in that place to pick guavas. I had never before eaten so many guavas. They were sweet beyond sweetness.

"They will come past the guavas in returning to the cave," said my friends. "Be very still."

We hid behind a tree, and soon I heard a guttural muttering that must have been their speech. Soon they came up the path facing the tree where we were hiding, and I saw their faces.

128

They were short and quite fair. Both the men and the women had long hair made into pugs with sticks through them. They wore old trousers cut short, and one old woman also had a white T-shirt and bright red suspenders that caught my eye.

Then on the island of Hawai'i, I went to Puna to visit Mrs. Johansen. She is German and Hawaiian and keeps all the old customs. She prepared *poi* and dried fish for us. When it was ready, she said, "Let's take our plates to the *lānai* and eat there."

"For any special reason?" I inquired.

"Oh, I like to look out at the ocean," she said. "Besides, I am expecting some friends."

And so we did, sitting at an old-fashioned walnut table. As we ate, the dogs began barking and running toward the gate. She called them back and said, "My friends are coming."

I glanced toward the gate and saw two short figures. "They are very small. Are they your neighbor's children?"

"They are not children at all," she said, laughing. "Wait, and you will see."

They approached her and said, *"Aloha,"* making a strange guttural noise in their throats.

She greeted them kindly and asked, "Where is your friend?" holding up three fingers. They made signs that their friend was asleep. Then she motioned for them to come sit and eat at the table, but they went under the table, holding up their cupped hands. Into their hands she put the fish, then gave each of them a calabash of *poi.* They ate, talking quietly among themselves with the strange speech I had never heard before.

"Who are they?" I asked softly. "What kind of people are they?"

"They are Hawaiian," said my friend.

"No, no," I said. "They are not Hawaiian. They are the Menehune, the short people who were here before the coming of the Hawaiians from across the sea."

She laughed, "Oh no, indeed, Harriet. They are Hawaiians. When I

130

work in my taro patch, they come silently up to me. I tell them what I want done and the next day it is so, even as I described it. One of my taro patches has a spring in it which opens into the ocean. Whenever I want a special kind of fish, I send one of them down into the water of the spring and he comes back with the fish. Perhaps he swims through to the ocean to bring it."

I was astonished. "I have heard that the Menehune will not go in water above their waists because they fear it."

"Then they are not Menehune," she said, "for this one will dive into the spring to the ocean and bring back my fish. You don't believe me? I'll tell him to do so."

She spoke to them in Hawaiian and they seemed to understand, their eyebrows going up when they were puzzled, their eyes lighting up when they understood. When she repeated it again, their eyes twinkled and they laughed low in their throat, "heh, heh, heh, heh," and ran away. And indeed they came back some time later bearing the fish that Mrs. Johansen loved.

And that is how I saw the Menehune.

The Five Red Rays
of Kalamaʻula

This is a tale of the old days that took place at the famous stone of Kalamaʻula.

In a small village towards the seashore lived a beautiful chief's daughter. She had given her love to a fine young man, but he was not noble. He lived way up by Nānāhoa, and they met often at a rendezvous spot marked by a large stone. Always, the daughter's *kahu keiki*, or nurse, would attend them.

When the chief discovered that his daughter had deceived him and fallen in love with a commoner, he was very angry, for Hawaiian law forbade such a marriage. He forbade her to see her lover again, even though she pleaded for his approval and declared that her love was unchangeable.

So strong was her love that she disobeyed her father and continued to meet with the boy. The chief then called the young man to him. "I do not doubt your love for my daughter nor hers for you," he said. "But you know the law. Nothing can come of this. You must end this and go away at once."

132

The young man bowed his head. "I know that what you say is true," he said. "I know I have done wrong in continuing to meet her, even though we have broken no *kapu* and she is still a maiden. I will do as you say, but we have already planned to meet this night. I promise that I will say goodbye if you will give me your permission to see her one more time."

But the chief would not give his permission, and so great was the young man's respect that he would not disobey the chief.

And so it was that the girl and her *kahu keiki* arrived at the rendezvous stone and waited that night. Long they watched and waited. When he did not come, the *kahu keiki* implored, "He is not coming. Surely he will not come. Let us return."

"I shall not return," said the girl determinedly. "I shall sleep right here on this stone. If he comes or sends word, you must wake me." And so, wearied by watching and worry, she slept.

No lover's voice or lover's touch awoke her, and she did not stir until the red rays of the sun touched her eyes. Everything around her was pure and clear. Immediately she asked, "Did he come? Why did you not waken me?"

Sadly her *kahu keiki* answered, "He did not come."

Suddenly, smitten by grief, the girl knew that he would never come again. She turned to gaze at the rock where she had slept and struck it. "I now call you Kalama'ula, because five red rays, and not my lover, woke me this morning," she cried. "This stone must remain here forever." Immediately the five red rays burned themselves permanently into the stone.

That was long ago and that is how Kalama'ula got its name. But not so long ago, a road overseer came along the path of a new road and told his men to remove the stone. At first they tried to dig it up, but that proved to be impossible.

"We must use dynamite," the workmen reported.

They dug a hole and placed three sticks of dynamite in it, then decided to eat their lunch and sat down in the shade. The overseer

133

went off to eat with his aunt, Bertha Meyer, who is now ninety-two years old. When he told her about the morning's work and said that the Kalama'ula rock must be removed with dynamite for the roadway, she became alarmed.

"Oh no, my boy, don't do that" she cried. "A powerful *kapu* is attached to it. Please don't destroy the rock." Then she told him the story of the five red rays.

Quickly understanding her alarm, he said, "But the men may already have blasted it." Even though he had not finished eating, he returned quickly to the rock. Fortunately the men were still eating. When he had told them the story of the Kalama'ula rock, they all agreed that it was sacred, a place of power.

I myself have seen this rock.

Some years after that, a tourist came to visit the place. She had a chisel and hammer in her bag and began to chisel one of the five rays from the surface of the rock. I scolded her and made her stop. Even though the rock is old and crumbling, you can still see the marks of her chisel. Now tall grass surrounds it and a pipe railing fence protects it.

There is a song about the rock and its story. And there is a story about the song. I will tell you this story. Long ago, long after the beautiful chief's daughter, the family whose lands held the rock composed a chant about it and about the lovers.

Many years later, a woman in the family named Emma, the mother of a friend, composed a song about it. The first verse sings of the beauty of the place.

Sometimes when I sing that verse, people are confused. "What beauty?" they say.

Always I answer, "Your eyes see no beauty, but to the *kama'āinas*, the land and the stones—all is beautiful to them."

The second verse tells the story of the chief's daughter and her lover. Emma turned it into a popular song. She did well. But she wanted to make it longer, so she took the words from the old chant of the five red rays and added them to this popular song. In this, she did not do well. A growth came on her throat. Perhaps it was goiter, but it closed up her windpipe so that she could hardly breathe.

The grandmother of my husband, Tūtū Luka, used to live on the hill above the rock. She was a *hoʻōla*, a healer, and very wise. Emma's family brought her to my husband's grandmother.

The wise grandmother opened her Bible so that its healing power would be present, and she asked Emma, "Have you eaten anything forbidden? Have you said anything forbidden?"

"No," said the woman, "but I am composing a song." She sang the first two verses and her voice came freely. "But I want to make it longer," she said, "and so I am adding some of the words of the chant."

Tūtū Luka understood at once. "That is what you must not do. The chant is by the family. It must stay in the family, not be sung by anyone in any place. You are a member of the family and the chant is yours also, but you cannot take the chant and put it into a modern song for others to sing. Nor may you sing it in public. It is permitted to sing just among your family."

So Emma obeyed and wrote her song only with the two modern verses but with no words from the chant. The tightness in her throat disappeared.

Many months later at a *lūʻau* for the seventy-fifth birthday of a respected aunt, the whole neighborhood came. Emma also was there, and they asked, "Emma, please sing for us."

She stood and she sang the song, but instead of stopping at the end of the modern verses, she continued into the chant. Even as she sang, she felt the muscles in her throat constrict until her breath stopped. She could not go on. She fell from the table where she was standing.

Quickly they brought her to Tūtū Luka and told her what had happened. "You will not receive another chance," said the grandmother of my husband. "You must believe that the chant is just for the family."

135

This time, Emma listened to her and obeyed. She wrote down the song for her daughter to record, but she wrote only the modern version. She would not write the chant or even sing it for her daughter again lest misfortune befall her.

The song became popular. I have heard that the records sell very fast. But no one else knows about the chant and its power.

The Power
of Tūtū Luka

When there is an evil spirit in a person the ancient *kamaʻāina*s
would call for a *kahuna* to perform a *kipaku*, or a banishment of the
demons. Tūtū Luka, the grandmother of my husband, was a *hoʻōla*, a
healer, and very wise. She was a Christian and did her healing work
through a Bible.

People used to come to her with very bad sicknesses—like asthma
or heart trouble or tuberculosis. "The doctor says I will die," they
would say.

Tūtū Luka would say, "Sit here."

She would sit near the person, and soon she would get a strange
feeling. "Oh, ho!" she would exclaim. "It is not sickness but the devil
which is in you. You are possessed. Have you been baptized?"

Almost always, the person had indeed been baptized and would
say, "Yes."

"Then you belong to Christ," Tūtū Luka would say firmly. "Have
you accepted Jesus as your savior?"

Nearly always the person would say, "Yes."

137

"Then you have not been keeping yourself Christian," Tūtū Luka would announce. "You have not been going to church. You have not read your Bible. You have not kept Christ in your heart."

The person would be astonished and would confess, "Yes, that is so."

"That is why you have become ill," Tūtū Luka would say. "You have opened the doors so the devil could come into you and dwell in you because you have not been holy. I will cast this demon out of you."

Then she would take her Bible and put it on the head of the sick person, saying, "In the name of Jesus Christ." The demons within would be tormented by the presence of the Bible, which tells of Christ, and so the sick person would back away and try to push the Bible away.

But Tūtū Luka would pay no attention. In a loud voice she would pray, as she held the Bible in place. "I command you, demon, to depart," she would say. "And you, O woman, remember that the Lord is the only true God and that He is mighty in power. O Christ, cast out this evil. O Christ, hear our prayer. O Christ, heal this woman and make her whole."

My husband told me about one *kipaku* that he helped with when he was young. Because Tūtū Luka spoke only Hawaiian, he had to interpret to the people that came to her for help, even though he himself had only a fourth-grade education.

On this occasion, Tūtū Luka said to him, "You go stand by the door and when I raise my hand, you open the door."

He stood by the door and prayed in Hawaiian as she prayed. Then as she ordered the demon to depart, she raised her hand and he opened the door. In relating this experience to me, he said, "I felt something swoosh by me. I heard the sound. I felt the rush of air." Quickly he shut the door, but the ceremony was not over. Again his grandmother commanded the demons to depart. Again she raised her hand. Again he opened the door and felt something swish by him.

138

This portion of the ceremony was repeated seven times. When it was over and the afflicted woman, now quiet and healed, had gone, he asked his grandmother, "But how is it that we repeated the door-opening seven times? In the past, we have opened the door only once."

She responded, "This person had seven devils. Seven demons were in her. That's why she was so sick and weak. She was totally possessed of evil forces and was compelled to obey the demons in all things. Whatever inspiration she may have received from Jesus, she could not obey. She had not the strength, the energy. She had given her will to the demons and no longer had the ability to fight against them. She is free of their influence now; but if she is not watchful and prayerful, she may again open the door to them. This is a very dangerous time for her."

Tūtū Luka knew of the battle that went on constantly for human souls. That is why, after a *kipaku*, she would also have a cleansing blessing, putting the Bible on their heads again as they knelt and praying to God to cleanse the person both within and without from all desire to do evil.

She would also instruct the person strictly, "You must keep God in your heart all the time so that there will be no room for Satan to enter. Be strong. If he tells you to do something wrong, fight back. God gave you brains. You know which is right and which is wrong. If you know that it is wrong, don't do it. Don't be afraid of the devil. If you're afraid, he's going to take advantage of you. If you are confident in Christ, then He will bless you and defend you. Never fail to do good to others and to love one another."

And that was the power of Tūtū Luka. I myself have seen it.

The Horse Thief
of Hoʻolehua

At Hoʻolehua, near the airport, lived a boy named Isaac. He was polite to his elders, a kind-hearted boy, and a baptized Christian. But he made a mistake that allowed evil forces to possess him. I myself saw this boy during his dark hour.

This is how his temptation and his trial came upon him.

Across the road from Isaac lived a big man named Kiawe who owned horses. Isaac loved horses and always wanted to ride; but instead of asking Papa Kiawe if he could ride a horse, as he had in the past, he one day followed an evil impulse and stole the horse upon which his heart was set. He rode this horse up to Maunaloa, far away, tethered the horse, and gave it water and food.

He thought in his heart, Whenever I wish to ride the horse, I can come here. No one will know. I will reveal my secret to no one. And thus he returned home.

But as he began walking up the steps of his house, something kicked him with terrible force, just like the hoof of a horse. He rolled off the steps to the earth in great pain, crying out for his mother.

When she opened his shirt, the print of a hoof was plainly visible on his chest.

His mother was astonished and frightened. "What have you done?" she cried.

Even with the hoof print before his eyes and the terrible pain cutting his breath, Isaac lied and said, "I have done nothing. I understand nothing."

She was a wise woman and said, "This is not an ordinary sickness. No doctor can help you."

She sent for Dr. Hansen, a *kama'āina* doctor who was trained in American medicine but who also knew ancient lore. When he saw the hoof print on Isaac's chest, he said at once, "A *kahuna* has done this." Turning to the mother, he explained, "This boy has done something wrong, something which brought upon him the wrath of a *kahuna*. And it's something to do with a horse."

At those words, the boy writhed in pain and, as if the words were forced from him, gasped, "It is so. I stole Papa Kiawe's horse and rode it to Maunaloa. It is hidden there."

The mother exclaimed, "Why did you do that? Why didn't you go ask him for permission to ride the horse?"

Isaac twisted his face away and said, ashamed, "He would not have given permission. He is a mean man."

Dr. Hansen said gravely, "This is a serious matter. You must call Papa Aiao to come, for he has the most knowledge of how to fight the power of the *kahuna*."

Now Papa Aiao was my father. He was a good Christian with much faith, and his power had been stronger than that of many *kāhuna* in the past. I was at the house when Isaac's mother telephoned, asking him to come and *ho'oponopono*, or put things to right. I heard my father say he would go, and immediately I began begging for permission to accompany him. At last he agreed. "You may come, daughter, but you must remain in the truck, for this is *kahuna* business."

141

When we reached Isaac's house, he repeated his orders that I must remain in the truck. I nodded seriously, but I could hear Isaac's mother wailing and wailing. My curiosity overpowered me, and I left the truck and crept to the steps behind the door. There I heard my father's voice question Isaac in Hawaiian. Isaac did not speak Hawaiian, so when a voice answered in Hawaiian, my father knew at once that it was the work of a *kahuna*.

Then he asked, " *'O wai 'oe?"* (Who are you?)

In a voice not like his own and speaking in Hawaiian, Isaac answered, "Kiawe."

"What do you want with this boy?"

Again the voice replied, "Isaac stole my horse, so he is going to be like a horse for the rest of his life. He will bear my mark and he will go on all fours for the rest of his life."

"No," said my father with great authority. "He cannot. It is impossible. You cannot have him because he has been baptized in the name of Jesus Christ. His God is Jesus Christ."

At these words, Isaac started up violently. His family seized him to hold him, but Isaac whirled and kicked backwards like a horse, striking his older brother with such force that he knocked the brother down. The brother started up angrily, but my father calmed him with soothing words. "It is not he but the demon within him which does this."

Again my father said to the evil one, "You have no authority over this boy. He has done wrong, but he belongs to Jesus Christ and he will make restitution. You must leave him."

The power of the *kahuna* ebbed and flowed like waves. For a time, Isaac would sit peaceably, answering sensibly when my father asked him questions and recalling the teachings of his church.

To cast out the *kahuna*, my father asked him in Hawaiian, "Do you remember some of the verses in the Bible? Recite the ones that you know." And the *kahuna*, bound by the power of Jesus Christ, would be obliged to say the holy words.

But then with a great effort, the *kahuna* would reassert his posses-
sion of Isaac, and he would roll and neigh and kick like a horse. During one of these times, he came bursting out the door, followed by the
entire family. I was afraid that my father would see me, but he had
eyes only for Isaac, who galloped around the yard and then settled
down to crop grass, exactly like a horse. I stared with all my eyes. I
could see that he was a boy, but he behaved so exactly like a horse
that I was filled with amazement.

My father was unable to make the *kahuna* respond while Isaac did
this, so he spoke quietly to the family. "I must rest for a time before
we can begin again, but the grass here has been sprayed with insecti-
cide. Help me bring him to my home where the grass is clean."

With their assistance, we brought him home in our truck and he
snorted, pawing at the grass, then settling down once more to crop it.
He would raise his head and whinny, shaking his lips and foaming at
his nose.

I was dumbfounded. How can this be? I wondered. I did a disre-
spectful thing. I went over to him and shouted "Whoa! Whoa!"

My father nudged me sharply and sent me back to the house, so I
sat very quietly on the steps and did not move, for I wished greatly to
see what would happen.

After my father had rested for a little while and prayed apart, he
came back to Isaac and began praying, again and again commanding
the *kahuna* to release the boy and depart, reciting the promises of
Jesus Christ to the believers and ordering the demon to depart. It
seemed that he went on for hours.

Then suddenly, Isaac fell down backward on the grass, completely
exhausted.

My father also was very tired. "It is over," he told Isaac's family.
"The devil has left his body. The curse has gone. We can take him
home. Give him a warm bath. Feed him and put him to sleep. But
don't give him anything with bones. He might choke. His body isn't
functioning correctly."

143

Isaac did not stir while we put him in the truck and drove him back to his home. "We will give him rice soup and put him to bed," said the mother, "but I am very afraid. Please don't leave. What if the spirit comes back?"

"It is possible that he may try," said my father, "but you have the power yourself. You must pray. Hold Isaac's hand. Both of you pray. And in all your prayers, call upon Jesus Christ. He is the true God, more powerful than the *kahuna,* and He has promised to deliver you. But you must no longer do evil, and Isaac must bring the horse back tomorrow and apologize to Papa Kiawe."

And so it was. That boy is perhaps fifty years old now. He lives on Kaua'i. We do not meet often; but when we do, he greets me with tears in his eyes, weeping for gratitude because he remembers my father.

The Healing

This is another tale of my father and how he battled against the ancient demons of Hawai'i through his faith in Jesus Christ.

It happened that one year my father went to the island of Hawai'i to do missionary work and took my mother and me with him. He spent as much time as he could spare from his work telling people about Jesus, but he did not stay in the big cities. He would go to the villages and into the fields, into isolated places. And we went with him.

We were in our car driving to Puna when he passed a certain house, a high house, old and unpainted. Suddenly he stopped, backed up, and parked. "We are going in here," he said. "We must pray with the people in the house."

A man was sitting on the porch mending his nets with three dogs lying about him. He looked at us and went on with his work. As we came up to the front gate, the dogs charged down towards us barking. My mother hung back and said, "Oh, these people are not truly Hawaiian. The man did not greet us or call us to come in or even say

145

'aloha' or *'Pehea 'ōlua?'* (How are you?). He isn't even calling off the dogs."

But my father said, "Do not be afraid. We are going in the name of Jesus Christ."

I clung to my mother in fear, but my father opened the gate and we walked in. The great dog who led the other dogs stopped and growled at my father but did nothing more. The little one leaped over both the medium-sized dog and the big dog and sank his teeth into my father's leg. With the Bible in his hand my father pushed the dog away, and at once the dog seized the Bible, growling savagely. (I still have the Bible with all of the dog's teeth marks in it.)

And still the man on the porch did not move or call away the dogs.

My mother said, "Oh, let us go to the car. Let us go at once. Think of the child."

But my father was firm. "Do not these actions show clearly how they need God's help?" he said. "We must tell him the good news. We must tell him about God and about His great love."

My mother was pulling me toward the car; but despite my fear, I said, "No, Mama. I want to go in. I want to see who also lives inside that house."

The dogs were still growling but no longer attacked my father, so we all approached the steps and began to climb the stairs. Still, the man refused to look up from his work or to speak. Never before had I seen a Hawaiian behave in such a strange way.

My father called, *"Hūi, hūi!"* and, in Hawaiian, "Where are the people of the house?"

From inside came a woman's voice calling, " *'Ae,* come in, come in."

My father looked at the man. "Well?" he inquired. The man, who must have been the head of the house, said nothing and did not look at us.

To my mother, such behavior was frightening. "Oh, let us go immediately away," she begged. She turned to walk down the steps and the smallest dog leaped from underneath the big dog and seized her foot. She was wearing tough leather shoes and quickly shook the dog off, stepping backwards up the steps until she stood by my father.

"You see," said my father. He was smiling. "God wishes you to stay. Let us stay and do His will."

So without looking again at the silent man, he opened the screen door and we walked into the living room. It was dark and a strange smell, like sulfur, lingered on the air, making it heavy.

My father sniffed once and said, "So it is true. These people worship Pele."

He pointed. I turned and saw an image carved in wood like a tiki, sitting on the table in the corner. Its eyes were made of mother-of-pearl. Even as I looked, the eyes moved, rolling up, then looking at me! Even as I looked, the tongue protruded.

I backed up against my mother. "It looks at me," I cried.

"Come," she whispered. "We must leave this place at once."

"No, we must stay," said my father. "Do not be afraid. Jesus Christ is stronger than Pele."

The woman's voice called again, *"Hele mai, hele mai"* (Come, come). All of us walked toward the voice and into a bedroom. A terrible odor of sickness greeted us. She was lying on the bed covered with rags soaked with pus. We could see an open wound on her side. The bed was foul with excrement and pus.

But my father did not flinch or hesitate. In Hawaiian he told her who we were. "We are servants of God. We have come to give you good news of Jesus Christ in His holy book. It is cancer that devours you, is it not?"

"Yes, she said, "and *pohopoho*" (an open, infected wound).

Looking with compassion upon her, he asked, "How long have you been sick?"

"It is eighteen years," she said.

"Have you gone to see the doctor?" he asked.

"No," she said. "My husband does not permit it. How is it that he

147

allowed you to enter? He does not believe in Jesus Christ. He does not permit Christians to come in. He does not allow anyone to talk to me about the Bible or about the word of God."

"Should we leave?" asked my father.

"No," she cried. "I want you. He is the head of the house, but I want you to stay." She gripped my father's hand, weeping. "Please pray for me."

So my father prayed for her, holding her hand. He sat in a chair beside the bed and read to her in Hawaiian from the Bible. I watched her face. After a time, she stopped crying and the terrible lines of pain in her face began to relax.

Quietly my father told my mother, "Please go outside and ask the man if you can bathe his wife." For this woman told us she couldn't remember when she had last had a bath. "Cleanliness is like God," said my father. "Please, permit us to bathe you and put you in a clean bed."

My mother returned. "He has not forbidden it." The sick woman again began to cry with tears that did not cease.

My father sent my mother out to look in the trunk of the car for a nightgown and some sheets. She found an old flannel nightgown. It had many rents and tears, but it was clean.

There was no bathroom in the house. I found a pan and a bucket in the yard and a tub hanging on the back of the house. My father brought it into the bedroom, and I went back and forth to the kitchen sink, filling it up with warm water. I think it took eight buckets to fill the tub almost to the three-quarters mark.

When all was ready, my father said, "I will wait outside the bedroom, praying until you are finished."

My mother and I closed the door and each of us took a hand to help the woman sit up. The stench of her illness rose in waves with her. When I pulled the scraps of her nightgown from her back, the skin seemed to come with it, blackened until it no longer looked like flesh.

I started to say something, but my mother shook her head sternly

148

at me, and I helped in silence. My mother had been trained in a nursing home to help sick people and knew what to do. We rolled the woman to one side and laid a clean towel beneath her. Then with warm water and soap, we gently rubbed the woman's skin. Because my mother had been in an accident when she was young, her knee was stiff and she couldn't bend over far. She would wring out the cloths for me and I would lean over the woman, rubbing gently until the dirt disappeared. First one side, then the other side, first washing, then rinsing.

At that time, I loved the smell of baby powder and always carried a can with me. I ran out to the car and took it from the front seat where I had left it, then brought it in. When the woman was dry, we put the powder on her arms and body and under her arms. The smell of soap and the powder began to make a sweeter smell in that room of sickness.

And so we washed her, first one side, then the other side. With the help of my father, we threw away the water and brought clean water to wash her wound and her feet in a separate step. As we worked, my father continued to pray, his voice rising and falling in Hawaiian outside the door. And even as he prayed, the pus stopped oozing from the wound and the edges began to draw together. Even before our eyes, we saw the healing begin.

My mother bandaged the wound with clean compresses. Then we dressed the woman in the clean nightgown and, with my father's help, rolled her to one side so we could change the sheet. There were no clean pillow cases, so I wrapped part of a sheet around the pillow. We laid her back down again in a clean, fresh bed, and my father propped her up against the pillow.

"Oh thank you, thank you," she kept saying.

When we were finished, she asked my father to lift up the mattress at her feet. She leaned over and pulled out some newspapers. Within the sheets of paper were bills, five-dollar bills and ten-dollar bills. She took a ten-dollar bill and gave it to me.

"No, no, no," I said. "You cannot give me money."

"You must take it," she said. "It is nothing for the work you have done for me."

Again I said, "No, no, no. We did it for the Lord because we love you."

"But you do not know me," she said. "How is it possible?"

"We don't have to know you," I responded. "We know that God made you, so we are all sisters."

"Please," she said, "take this for you."

Again I refused, but she kept holding my hand and trying to put the money into it, weeping.

At last, I said, "I will take the money and give it to the church. The church can use it for other work."

My father smiled at me, then held the woman's hand and blessed the money that she was giving to me. She had a Protestant hymnal in the room, so we all sang hymns. She sang with great happiness, hymn after hymn. At the sound of the singing, her husband came and stood by the door, his hands on hips and a dark look on his face.

In Hawaiian, she said, "Go, leave us alone. Do not send them away. They have made me happy."

So he walked away.

At last we said, "We must leave now."

Again tears came to her eyes. "I wish I could get up to get you something to eat."

"Thank you," said my father. "You are kind, but we have already eaten."

We left the house. The man was nowhere to be seen. As we went through the gate, I said, "Papa, I feel awful. May I wash my hands?"

He said I could and I went to the faucet in the yard. As I scrubbed my hands with soap to wash away the last smell of the pus and dirt, a hot, black loop snaked up from the hole where the pipe disappeared into the ground and wrapped around my ankle. It was black Pele's hair.

I screamed. My father ran to me and saw at once what it was. Quickly he brought his Bible from the car and commanded in Hawaiian, "Release her!" The thing recoiled and withdrew into the hole.

I ran to the car. My mother looked at my ankle. It was red, red, red, stinging and burning. From the side of the road, my mother gathered aloe vera leaves and rubbed the soft, cool gel from inside the leaves on my ankle. The heat and pain disappeared at once.

As we drove away, my father said, "What an experience!" My mother and I agreed with all our hearts.

My father looked at my mother and smiled. "You know, you must ask God to forgive you for wanting to leave because He had a work for us to do there. As I passed this house, I felt constrained by the Holy Spirit. I knew that we must enter that house."

My mother said, "It is so," and her lips moved in a silent prayer.

I was happy that I had been with them, for I had learned a great many things that day. My father looked at me and said kindly, "This has been a great deal of work for you. You may lie down on the back seat and sleep."

Just as I was drifting off, something came into my mind and I cried, "Oh Papa, stop! We must go back. I left my can of powder there."

"Will you not leave it with that woman?" he asked. "I know she will cherish it. She has so little of cleanliness and comfort."

I began to cry, for I knew it was true. "Yes, Papa," I said. "She may have it."

He smiled at me and I went to sleep. When I woke, we were stopped in Hilo and he had just gone into the store. When he came out, in his hand he held another can of baby powder.

The Reconciliation

This is how the breach in a family that I myself knew was healed.

It was a family of three children with wide lands and a large fish farm. After the father died, the mother became ill, her body aching hour by hour through the days and nights. The youngest child, a daughter named Anna, cared for her; but the son and other daughter did not wish to see her. The mother grieved especially because her son cared nothing for her.

Before she died, she told Anna, "This house and the fish farm will be yours. The four acres on the *mauka* side of the fishpond will be Mary's, and Kimo may have the car and whatever money I have in the bank."

Soon she died. After the funeral, Anna told them her mother's instructions. The brother was suspicious. "What money? I never knew she had money in the bank."

"I did not either," said Anna. "Not until she told me."

"Ah," he sneered. "You must have known. That is why you took care of her—to eat up her money."

Anna felt as if her heart would break. She wept and wept. She turned away from her brother and refused to speak another word to him, and from that day they did not speak to each other.

It was eighteen years later that I came to Anna. In those days, I would take my Bible and go out among the houses, inquiring if I could enter and study the Bible with the people of the house.

On this certain day, I came to Anna's house where I had been before to study the Bible with her. When I saw her face, I said, "Are you well? You seem ill."

She responded, "I believe that I have a sickness. My chest feels heavy and I am short of breath."

"Do you have heart trouble?" I asked.

"I don't think so," she said. "I just had a physical and the doctor said nothing."

"Why then do you feel ill?" I inquired.

"There is no reason," she said. "I am burdened, yes, heavily burdened."

"What is your burden?"

"I do not know," she said and sighed. "Nothing is wrong. I do not know why I feel so burdened."

Just then a car stopped outside and a friend of ours came in. He greeted us both, kissing me. "Hello, Anna. Hello, Auntie Harriet."

We talked for a few minutes, and Anna asked him to stay longer. "No," he said, "in the car is Kimo."

I was curious. "Why does he not come in also?"

Anna looked darkly at me and said, "I do not wish him to enter my house."

I felt the heaviness of which she had spoken. "What is it, Anna?" I asked gently.

"We have not spoken for eighteen years," she said.

"That is your burden, Anna," I said. "That is the heaviness in your heart. You are divided against yourself because you are divided against your brother."

She told me the story of her mother's death. "He did not believe that I spoke the truth," she said, "and now he wants the fish farm because he is greedy and wants more money."

Now, Anna herself had never fished from the ponds or sold the fish but had left them to grow stagnant and overgrown.

I sighed. "Please call him in so that he can join us in the prayer to close our Bible study."

"No!" she exclaimed. "Oh, no."

I went to the door and beckoned to him. "Kimo, please come in."

We had never had hard words, and he said pleasantly, "I do not wish to come if I will not be welcome."

"Erase that thought from your mind," I urged. "What is past is past. This is a new year. Forget the argument and begin to live a new life."

Slowly he got out of the car and approached until he was standing on the top step. There he stood.

I understood and turned inside to Anna. "He will not come until you call. Please invite him in."

She hesitated for a long moment, then said, "Kimo, come."

It was not a warm invitation but she had said the words, so he entered the house. As soon as he entered, I took his hand and said, "Now we will hold hands and pray."

He laughed and pulled his hand away. "What is this?"

"It is the closing of our Bible study," I said. "Today we studied humility. Anna told the beautiful story of the publican and the Pharisee."

Anna turned her face away.

In Hawaiian, I said, "Blessed is he that practices the teachings of the Lord. Come, give me your hands."

Slowly, they put out their hands, and we all clasped hands as we prayed. I offered the prayer, making a particular petition: "Please touch the hearts of both brother and sister."

Today they are the best of friends. They share. When he fishes, he brings part of his catch to her; and she has told him with goodwill, "You may come to the fishponds as you will. And if your church is going to have a money-making project, bring some of the men and fish in the ponds and sell the fish."

Now the brother and sister are happy. And I, too, am happy.

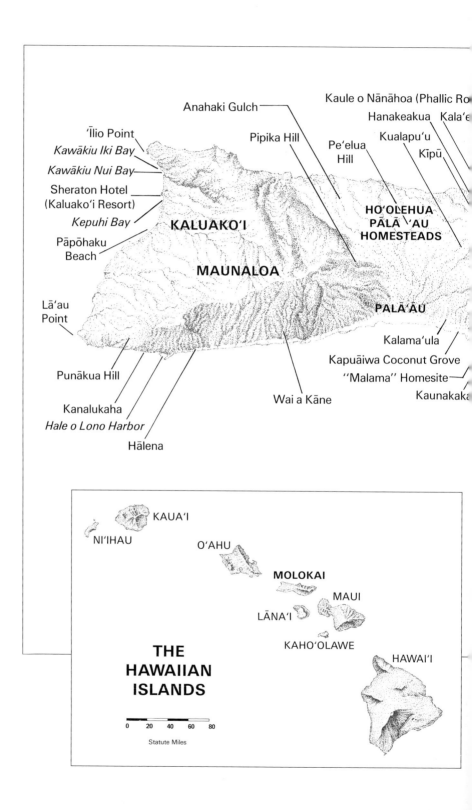

Anahaki Gulch

Kaule o Nānāhoa (Phallic Ro

Hanakeakua   Kala'e

'Īlio Point

Pipika Hill

Kualapu'u

Kawākiu Iki Bay

Pe'elua
Hill

Kīpū

Kawākiu Nui Bay

Sheraton Hotel
(Kaluako'i Resort)

Kepuhi Bay

KALUAKO'I

HO'OLEHUA
PĀLĀ 'AU
HOMESTEADS

Pāpōhaku
Beach

MAUNALOA

Lā'au
Point

PALĀ'AU

Kalama'ula

Kapuāiwa Coconut Grove

Punākua Hill

"Malama" Homesite

Kaunakaka

Wai a Kāne

Kanalukaha

Hale o Lono Harbor

Hālena

KAUA'I

NI'IHAU

O'AHU

MOLOKAI

MAUI

LĀNA'I

KAHO'OLAWE

HAWAI'I

THE
HAWAIIAN
ISLANDS

0   20   40   60   80

Statute Miles

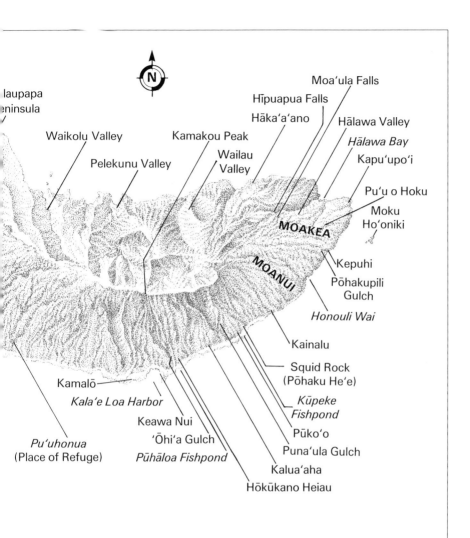

laupapa
:ninsula
/

Waikolu Valley

Pelekunu Valley

Kamakou Peak

Wailau
Valley

MOAKEA

MOANUI

Moa'ula Falls

Hīpuapua Falls

Hāka'a'ano

Hālawa Valley

Hālawa Bay

Kapu'upo'i

Pu'u o Hoku

Moku
Ho'oniki

Kepuhi

Pōhakupili
Gulch

Honouli Wai

Kainalu

Squid Rock
(Pōhaku He'e)

*Kūpeke
Fishpond*

Pūko'o

Puna'ula Gulch

Kamalō

Kala'e Loa Harbor

Keawa Nui

'Ōhi'a Gulch

Pu'uhonua
(Place of Refuge)

Pūhāloa Fishpond

Kalua'aha

Hōkūkano Heiau

Molokai

0   1   2   3   4   5   6

Statute Miles

Glossary

Terms are Hawaiian unless otherwise noted. The glottal stop (') is similar to the stopping of sound between the *oh*'s in the English *oh-oh*. Macrons denote long stressed vowels (ā, ē, etc.).

'ae yes
a'e soapberry tree
āholehole young *āhole*, the Hawaiian flagtail or silver perch, an endemic fish found in both fresh and salt water
'aiea a native soft-wooded tree
aku bonito, a medium-sized tuna
'alā dense water-worn volcanic stone; basalt
'alaea a kind of ocherous earth used for medicine
ali'i a chief or chiefess, noble, royal, aristocrat
ali'i nui high chief
aloha a loving greeting or farewell; love; sympathy, caring, sharing, hospitality

'ama'ama mullet
'aumakua family or personal god; deified ancestor
auwē Oh! Alas! Too bad! An exclamation of surprise, dismay, fear, sorrow, etc.
'awapuhi wild ginger, a forest herb
'āwikiwiki a native vine with narrow pods
ehuehu a kind of rock used to make adzes and axes
eō "Yes, I am here"
haki to break, snap, or fracture
hālau a longhouse, as for canoes or *hula* instruction
hālau wa'a canoe longhouse
hale house or building
hānai foster or adopted child; to foster or adopt
haole Caucasian, white person; foreigner
hau a lowland tree of the hibiscus family with a light, tough wood, formerly used for outriggers
heiau temple or place of worship
hele mai "Come in!" or "Come here!"
hīhīwai a type of shellfish
Hina name of a goddess or demigoddess. Many Hinas are widely known throughout Polynesia
hinahina native heliotrope, a low beach plant used for tea and medicine
hō'ike convention or gathering of Sunday schools with singing and dancing
ho'ōla healer
ho'oponopono to put things right; family conferences in which relationships are healed through prayer, discussion, repentence, and forgiveness
hūi "Hallo!"
hula a type of dance; to move to rhythmic song or chant
hula ku'i the punch *(ku'i)* hula of Molokai, a fast dance with doubling of fists as in boxing, heel twisting, thigh slapping, dipping of

knees, vigorous gestures imitative of such pursuits as dragging fish-
nets, and unaccompanied by instruments

'iao silversides, a small fish found in shallow pools

'ilima a type of flowering shrub related to the hibiscus

imu cooking pit, ground oven

kahakai sea water

kahu attendant, guardian, caretaker; reverend or pastor

kahu keiki one who tends a child as a nurse or attendant

kahuna (pl.: *kāhuna*) priest, sorcerer; expert or skilled person in any
profession

kahuna lapa'au curing expert, healer; a medicinal herb doctor

kahuna nui high priest and councilor to a high chief

kala a type of surgeonfish, also called bluespine unicornfish

Kalawina (from Eng.) Calvinism

kālua baked; to bake in a pit or underground oven

kama'āina one born in a place, lit., "child of the land"; long-time resident in an area, or resident from former times; an old-timer

Kanaloa one of the four major Hawaiian gods; many consider him
the god of the ocean

kapaka (the) tobacco

kapu taboo, forbidden or ritually sacred

kauna name of a current; nobleman, count

ke ali'i "O chief" or "the chief"

kīhei rectangular shawl or cloak of tapa, worn over one shoulder and
knotted

kipaku exorcism; banishment of demons; to send or drive away

kō sugarcane

koa *Acacia koa,* largest of native Hawaiian forest trees, valued for
its fine reddish wood. Formerly used for canoes, surfboards, cala-
bashes, and so forth; now used for furniture and ukeleles

ko'a fishing shrine

kōlea Pacific golden plover

Ko'olau windward side

kope (from Eng.) coffee

Kū one of the four major Hawaiian gods, said to be the god of war and canoes

kukui candlenut tree, a large, extremely important soft-wooded tree of the spurge family used in many ways by the Hawaiians. It bears nuts whose oily kernels were burned for lighting and were also used to make a relish and medicines

kūlolo a pudding of grated taro and coconut

Kū Lua fourth day of the old lunar month

kūmū whitespot goatfish

kumu hula *hula* teacher

Kumulipo name of the Hawaiian creation chant

kumuone sandstone

kupua demigods or supernatural beings that can take several forms

kupuna (pl.: *kūpuna*) grandparent, great-uncle or great-aunt; ancestor, elder

lae point, cape, promontory

lānai open porch or veranda

lau hala pandanus leaf, used in plaiting mats, baskets, etc.

laulau a wrapped package of leaves containing fish or meat baked in a ground oven or steamed

limu general name for water plants, both salt and fresh; seaweed

lo'i paddies or dyked terraces for planting taro, etc.

lo'i kalo terraces for taro patches

lokolo'i kalo taro pond

loko wai freshwater ponds

Lono one of the four major Hawaiian gods, associated with agriculture and fertility

loulu lelo a native fan palm

lū'au feast

māhalo thank you

makahiki fall festival of thanksgiving and peace, celebrated with sports and religious activities

malo loincloth
mao a type of small fish
mana supernatural or divine power
manini the common reef surgeonfish, also called the convict tang
Māui Famous demigod and trickster
mauka inland, upland, toward the mountains
me'e hero or heroine; heroic, admired
milo a type of tree, related to the *hau*
moi threadfish
moi li'i young threadfish
mo'o lizard
mo'olelo story, tale, history, tradition, legend
mo'opuna grandchild, descendant
mu'umu'u loose-fitting dress
nehe a plant used to make tea, also called *kī nehe* or Spanish needle
'ōhi'a a common type of tree with hard wood
'ōhi'a 'ai the mountain-apple, a forest tree with apple-like fruit
'ō'io ladyfish, bonefish
'ōlapa a dance accompanied by chanting and drumming
'o'opu general name for small fish found near shore and in brackish
    and fresh water, such as gobies and blennies
'ōpae shrimp
'ōpelu mackerel scad
'opihi limpet, a marine mollusk eaten for food
pale 'ili undershirt; short-sleeved clinging cotton shirt
pali cliff, precipice
pā'ū woman's wrap-around skirt or sarong
pe'elua caterpillar or army worm
Pehea 'ōlua? How are you two?
Pele goddess of the volcano and of fire
Pele's hair (Eng.) bits of liquid thrown up by lava fountains during
    volcanic eruptions that freeze in the air to form slender, glassy fila-
    ments resembling hair

pohopoho an open, infected wound

poi paste made by pounding cooked taro (sometimes breadfruit) with water

pua young child, offspring, spawn, fry

pua āholehole young *āhole,* a species of fish found in both fresh and salt water

pua 'ama'ama young grey mullet

pua awa young milkfish

puka hole, opening, door

pū'olo bundle, packet, container

pūpū general name for marine and land shells

pu'u hill, peak, mound

pu'uhonua place of refuge

pu'uone sand-dune ponds

squid (Pidgin) often used to mean "octopus"

tapa (Eng., from Tahitian and Marquesan; Hawaiian: *kapa*) a coarse cloth made from the pounded bark of the paper mulberry tree, used for clothing, bedding, etc.

taro (Eng.; Hawaiian: *kalo*) a kind of vegetable long grown throughout the tropics for its starchy, edible root, a staple of the Hawaiian diet since ancient times

ti (Eng.; Hawaiian: *ki*) shrub with long leaves, a member of the lily family, used for wrapping food, making raincapes, thatching, and as a protection against evil

tiki (Eng., from Maori and Marquesan; Hawaiian: *ki'i*) a wood or stone image of a supernatural being

ti nehe See *nehe*

tūtū grandmother or grandfather; any relative or close friend of the grandparents' generation

tūtū wahine grandmother

'ulapapa slipper lobster

uliuli a kind of stone from which adzes are made

ung choi (Chinese) cabbage, Chinese cabbage, swamp cabbage

Index

For the meaning of italicized words, see the Glossary. Landforms are, unless otherwise noted, on Molokai.

165

Index

Index

Index

Index

169

Index

170

Index